A Guide to
Point

An Rubha, The Eye Peninsula, Isle of Lewis

Edited by Liz Chaplin

Produced by Urras Eaglais na h-Aoidhe in conjunction with Point Community Council

© 2014, Urras Eaglais na h-Aoidhe.

Urras Eaglais na h-Aoidhe is a
Company Limited by Guarantee (214629)
and Registered Scottish Charity (SC030892)

Cover photographs by Virtual Hebrides, Janet Cameron and Simon Riley.

ISBN: 978-0-9573015-1-1

POINT COMMUNITY COUNCIL
COMHAIRLE COIMHEARSNACHD AN RUDHA

Comhairle nan Eilean Siar

EÒRPA AGUS ALBA
Maoin Leasachaidh Roinnean na h-Eòrpa
Taisg san àm ri teachd

Designed and printed by Shore Print & Design Ltd
Office 4 Clinton's Yard, Rigs Road, Stornoway, Isle of Lewis HS1 2RF

CONTENTS

FOREWORD

This is an exciting time to be a Rubhach, or resident of the Eye Peninsula, to give Point its correct geographical name. With the opening of the new Sgoil an Rubha, a state-of-the-art school for all the primary children in the peninsula, the former school buildings at Aird and Knock became surplus to Council requirements. Point Community Council set up a Trust, Urras Storas an Rubha, to acquire these buildings for community use, and provide much-needed facilities for local residents and visitors.

The Knock site, right at the entrance to the area, has already been leased by the Urras prior to raising the money to buy the building outright later in the year. Facilities here include a shop and cafeteria, local heritage museum, interpretation centre for the historic Ui Church, and offices for the Rudhach newspaper and Point and Sandwick Power. When the PSP windfarm is up and running it will generate significant funds for community projects which will benefit the whole of the Western Isles, but principally the Point/Sandwick area.

On the somewhat larger Aird campus at the other end of the peninsula it is hoped to establish a much-needed site for caravans and motorhomes, an art studio, fast food outlet, possible bunkhouse accommodation, an information centre on the rich marine wildlife around our shores, and a permanent base for the Point Agricultural Society which hosts a highly successful show every summer. Tiumpanhead Community Association, which already owns part of the site, will also have extended premises and storage for the many community events they organise regularly.

Point has perhaps been rather overlooked by visitors to the island in the past, partly because of the lack of 'tourist' facilities, but with these developments it is hoped that many more people will come to appreciate the scenery, flora and fauna, and rich archaeological and social history of the area. For a full appreciation of the magnificent coastline with its wide panoramic vistas of the North Minch and mainland mountains, a complete circuit of the peninsula is recommended for keen walkers (see the Guide inside); for those with limited time it has been broken into five reasonably easy sections.

This Guidebook, jointly produced by the Ui Church Trust and Point Community Council, provides a comprehensive guide to this fascinating area, with detailed and authoritative chapters by local experts. This project owes a great debt of gratitude to fellow Urras member Liz Chaplin, who sourced and collated a very impressive range of contributions, and of course to the contributors themselves.

Enjoy your visit to Point!

Tom Clark
Vice-chair, Point Community Council

ACKNOWLEDGEMENTS

The idea of a guidebook for Point was developed jointly by Point Community Council and Urras Eaglais na h-Aoidhe. We are grateful to the Community Council for donating some of the money from Bayble and Garrabost Community Association funds and to the Outer Hebrides Small Business Assistance Scheme for a grant towards publication costs.

Very special thanks are due to everyone who contributed to this Guidebook - for their hard work and the thought they each gave to their chapters. What talent there is on Point! Also very warm appreciation to Helen Macdonald who not only drew the map, but also gave consistent attention to detail as the book came together.

Equal thanks must go to the photographers who donated their photographs to illustrate the Guidebook; the main contributors were:

Chris Murray	Eilidh Whiteford
Simon Riley	Helen Macdonald
Christeen Mackenzie	Chris & Graham www.virtualheb.co.uk
Mike Wood	Krystyna Pytasz
Janet Cameron	Lewis Shand
Judy Macdonald	John Murray
Carol Knott	

Thanks to Roy Cameron, IT Media Services for help with digitalising photographs, to Christine Morrison for the recipes for Barley Meal and to Tom Clark and Helen Macdonald for proof reading.

Every effort has been made to acknowledge and credit photographs correctly, but please accept my sincere apologies if there are omissions or mistakes.

On a personal note; I would particularly like to express my appreciation to Tom Clark, Point Community Council, Ken Roddy Mackay, Comhairle nan Eilean Siar and to my fellow directors on Urras Eaglais na h-Aoidhe without whose help and encouragement this Guidebook would not exist. The production of this book was a real community effort.

Liz Chaplin
Editor

INTRODUCTION
Liz Chaplin

Point (*Eye Peninsula or An Rubha*) is on the east coast of the Isle of Lewis. It is a small peninsula joined to the rest of the island by a narrow isthmus of golden sands one mile long and barely 100m wide. Point has a proud heritage and a distinctive character of its own. From the dramatic memorial cairn to the Aignish Rioters sitting prominently on the Braighe to the towering beacon of the Tiumpanhead lighthouse, Point is a place of beautiful scenery, remarkable history, stunning wildlife and vibrant communities.

Point is currently home to approximately 2,600 people, inhabiting 14 villages, or crofting townships, along the 11 mile length of the peninsula. Community spirit is strong and people work together to develop and maintain facilities such as community centres, a very successful Agricultural Show and the Point football pitch; there is a range of youth groups, senior citizen groups and a well supported football team. Gaelic is spoken by many in the area and people work to maintain the area's cultural heritage. Although most people are employed in Stornoway, crofting still plays a significant part in the way of life of many Rubhachs.

A popular ancient myth tells the story of how the people of Point saved the rest of the inhabitants of Lewis:

"Back in the mists of time, Point was a separate island to the rest of Lewis. One dark winter's night, a violent and ferocious storm pounded the west coast of Scotland. As the gigantic waves

Aerial view of the Braighe   Chris Murray

Aerial view of Point looking north east   Chris Murray

rashed and crashed, Lewis began to drift hopelessly out into the Atlantic. The people of Point saw this happening and braved the storm to get a rope across to Lewis and stopped it floating away. Over time, around that rope gathered seaweed, algae and sand which eventually accumulated so that an isthmus was formed between Point and Lewis. Thus, according to the myth, the people of Lewis owe a great debt to the inhabitants of Point for saving them that night."

Some examples of current initiatives in Point are:

Sgoil an Rubha

Point had three schools until 2011 in Knock, Garrabost (Bayble School) and Aird. In 2011 a new school - Sgoil an Rubha was built on the site of Bayble School to serve the whole of Point. The school has a Croileagan (Gaelic Nursery), an English speaking Nursery, mainstream classes from primaries 1 - 7 and a Gaelic Medium Unit. It has about 180 pupils and their website states: "In August 2011 we were delighted to move into a wonderful new state-of-the-art school which provides first-class facilities for learning and teaching. The building has received wonderful comments from the many visitors we have had and we are sure our new environment for learning will encourage and inspire pupils and staff on a daily basis. The school is definitely very well equipped to serve the pupils of the area well into the 21st century."

Point Community Council

The Community Council is an active body of local people who meet regularly with the three Councillors for Sgire an Rubha for the benefit of the local community. Over the years the Community Council has been responsible for initiating projects such as Urras

Images from Point Show   *Janet Cameron*

Eaglais na h-Aoidhe (Ui Church Trust) Point and Sandwick Development Trust Point First Responders and Urras Storas an Rubha (Point Development Trust).

Point Churches

Religion is an important part of many people's lives in Point. The Church of Scotland, the Free Church of Scotland and the Free Church of Scotland (Continuing) all have churches here and on the whole Sunday observance is part of the local culture.

Point Show

For many years the idea of a Point Show or some community event catering for all sections of the community was often mooted, but usually cast aside as being an impossible task. However, a community appraisal by Point Community Council demonstrated a strong wish for something like this which, coupled with a sense of belonging to a community entrenched in history, fuelled the energy that created the Point Agricultural Society.

In 2002 a small dedicated group of Rubhachs gathered together and constituted the Point Agricultural Society. They subsequently agonised, persevered, organised, begged, borrowed, encouraged and most of all succeeded in bringing the community together for the Inaugural Point Show in August 2003. Since then, the Show has continued to go from strength to strength and the Society celebrated its tenth Anniversary show in 2012.

Bùth an Rubha and Café Roo

Point shop and café were opened in March 2014 and are a 'must-see' for all visitors to Point. The facility includes a café, toilets and parking as well as a local heritage museum. The shop sells a wide variety of produce as well as local books, including Colin Scot Mackenzie's book on St Columba's U

Church, local crafts and leaflets on Point and Ui Church.

Community Newspaper

The 'Rudhach' is the monthly community newspaper for Point. With a committee of 11 dedicated individuals, some regular contributors and a network of 16 village correspondents, the Rudhach successfully reports on current news and events combined with a look at times gone by. In 2012 the Rudhach was named 'Community Newspaper of the Year' at the Highlands & Islands Media Awards.

Point and Sandwick Development Trust

The Trust is a community-owned company limited by guarantee and a registered charity, which was formed after a series of public meetings on Point in 2005 to discuss ways in which the community could benefit from renewable energy. The Board is elected by the members of the company at the AGM. All electors living in the Point and Sandwick districts of Lewis are entitled to join as members. There is no membership fee.

The Development Trust has a wholly-owned trading arm, Point and Sandwick Power which will build and operate a community owned 9MW wind farm at Beinn Ghrideag outside Stornoway. The net income from the wind farm (after deduction of costs) will be gift-aided to the Development Trust to use for the benefit of the local community in accordance with its Community Development Plan.

Urras Storas an Rubha

Point Development Trust has been established to enable the community to buy and manage the Knock and Aird School sites for the benefit of the community. The Knock site now houses Bùth an Rubha (the local shop), Café Roo, a local heritage museum run by Point Historical Society,

Point Show   *Janet Cameron*

Bùth an Rubha   *Liz Chaplin*

interpretation facilities for Ui Church and various offices. The Aird site is still being developed, but exciting possibilities are at the community consultation stage. These will enhance the already well established Aird Community Centre.

Comunn Eachdraidh an Rubha

Point Historical Society began in 1982 and has collected historical material from the whole of Point. The Society published a Roll of Honour 1939–1945. The Society has moved into the former Knock School where it holds exhibitions based around its museum and archive collections and interpretation of the Ui Church.

Urras Eaglais na h-Aoidhe

Ui Church Trust was established in 2001 to safeguard this beautiful medieval church at the eastern end of the Braighe on the shore of Broad Bay. The building has been stabilised and consolidated and it is once again open to the public - be sure to visit it.

The beauty of this Guidebook is that it is written by a wide variety of local people who know and love the district of Point. The chapters have been chosen to reflect the most significant aspects of Point, especially those of interest to visitors. Point may lack the magnificence of the Harris hills or the wild beauty of the Uig sands, but what it offers is a real, live community of people - both locals and incomers - who enjoy living here and who work together to maintain a sense of community. This guidebook gives an excellent insight into the social history, archaeology and natural history of a community living at the extreme edge of Europe.

Sunset over Broad Bay   *Simon Riley*

Ui Church from the shore　　　　　　　　　　　　　　　　　*Janet Cameron*

EAGLAIS NA H-AOIDHE/ ST COLUMBA'S CHURCH AT UI
Colin Scott Mackenzie

Whatever else you do, *wherever* else you go in the whole of the Western Isles do not fail to visit the ancient church dedicated to Colm Cille (St Columba, the quintessential spiritual leader of Gaeldom in both Scotland and Ireland). Its ruins have weathered all the many Hebridean storms since at least the 13th century. They are to be found situated at Ui - at the very start of what cartographers call the Eye Peninsula but which the natives call "An Rubha" (pro. 'roo' - anglicé 'Point').

What you now see, however, was not by any means the start of the story. There has been a Christian presence at Ui since as long ago as the 6th century of our era when St Catan built his monkish cell on site. At the time Lewis formed part of the Northern Pictish kingdom, though Gaelic influence *may* already have reached its shores and that long since. Gaelic or Pictish, Christianity made its own significant mark early on the islanders and the island and, just as is said to be the case on distant Iona, the dividing line at Ui, separating our all-too material reality from an all-pervading spirituality, is accordingly paper-thin. A period of quiet contemplation in the surroundings of its mossy stones would prove that for many.

Ui Church   *Helen Macdonald*

Ui Church   *Mike Wood*

View from Ui Church   *Liz Chaplin*

Ui Church from Broad Bay   *Simon Riley*

The Viking raids of the ninth and tenth centuries brought terror and misery to the Christian community in the islands. In Lewis a form of ethnic cleansing took place which simply disposed of the bulk of the adult male population, at least of those who were not of immediate use to the Northmen, all by way of an early 'final solution' or, alternatively, export to the slave markets at Bergen. The monks, however, it is now thought by some scholars, may have been tolerated as suppliers of foodstuffs to the raiders – for whatever else they were, the Vikings were definitely not farmers - which may account for the fact that while every single major placename in Lewis is of Norse origin, St Catan's memory lived on, even through the horrors of these long pagan years.

Relief would have eventually come to these presumed Christian remnants when, at the end of the 10th century (995 AD to be precise), the Norse lands, of which we in the Hebrides were then part, were converted or reconverted to Christianity, all at the point of a sword. Much church building soon followed over all these realms but we cannot yet tell exactly when an actual church building was erected on the site of Catan's cell at Ui. The oldest part of the building which you now see dates from the 13th century or possibly from the 12th. Dating is now made possible from an examination of the different kinds of mortar employed at different times comparing them with others of known date and provenance.

Curiously enough, we do not know when precisely the church at Ui was dedicated to St Columba – or indeed why – save that that good saint outshone all his contemporaries and rivals – and of course his history was written by an admirer and follower whereas the others, of whom there were many, including Catan, lapsed into obscurity! The dedication is first mentioned in a Papal letter in 1433 but presumably it must have been already well in place by that time.

The church itself speedily grew into a most important foundation. It was said to have been at one time the richest in the Western Isles and was also said to have been burned to the ground twice – but, whether these were accidental conflagrations or the intended consequences of the endemic piratical raidings of the era, we simply do not know.

From forming part of a Pictish kingdom, to being part of the Earldom of Orkney, to part of the Norse Kingdom of the Isles (then subordinate to the Kings of Norway), and then later under the Danish crown, the islands were finally transferred to Scottish sovereignty in 1266 following the Treaty of Perth - although so far as the church was concerned the Nordic connection was not broken until as late as 1537.

In the meantime there grew out of the now transferred Kingdom of the Isles what was in effect, if not in theory, still a more or less independent realm. That semi-state is known to history as the Lordship of the Isles. Its times were troubled, but Gaelic culture throve within it and certain families within the Lordship were recorded as advancing their own interests in land and power. In Lewis (and elsewhere) the Nicolsons were already prominent having been first subject to the Kings (even before Scotland joined us) and subsequently to the Lords of the Isles, and it was during that Nicolson period of dominance that the earliest church we know of would have been built at Ui.

The Kings of Scotland, however, always had an uneasy relationship with the Gaelic west even after they had acquired sovereignty and they only *finally* managed to impose their supremacy (after much intrigue and many battles) in 1493 when they absorbed the title of the Lord of the Isles in the crown. Unfortunately the Kings did not thereafter for far too long introduce any proper form of governance in these realms and utter chaos then resulted in the former territories, including Lewis, as well as everywhere else. For self-protection and self-interest, families, and those connected with them, formed out of the ruins of society, what we know now as 'clans' – from the Gaelic 'clann' for children – the inference being that those who bore the same name were all mutually related. That however, was not necessarily so, as many outsider supporters would follow a successful leader and claim the name of the immediate family, though they might have had no direct blood relationship. Each clan had its own specific areas of influence and rivalry was intense. Initially it was the Wild West with a vengeance. Clans strove with clans, families with families; raiding between them was endemic and life was hard and often all too short.

Grave marker of Margaret Mackinnon, daughter of Roderick Macleod of Lewis and widow of Lachlan Mackinnon, who died in 1503, artwork by Helen Macdonald

Grave marker of Roderick Macleod, 7th Chief of Macleod, artwork by Helen Macdonald

One family in particular which grew to prominence even in the time of the Nicolsons' ascendancy were the descendants of Leod - possibly a grandson of the Norse King Olaf 'the Black' - of Man and the Isles. They were and are called the 'Macleods' – 'mac' being the Gaelic for 'son'. There are two branches of that clan, the *possibly* elder one said to be of Harris and the *probably* junior, if more numerous, of Lewis - though in fact they were always, so far as we can tell, of equal status in the region. The Lewis Macleods were also known as the 'siol Torcuil' – the seed of Torquil' – to distinguish them from the 'siol Thormoid' or Norman's seed, of Harris.

These Lewis Macleods succeeded the Nicolsons as superiors of the island of Lewis, in or about the end of the 14th century, according to their own tradition, by simple dint of their third chieftain, Murdoch, disposing of the Nicolson nearer heirs in one fell swoop in a boating 'accident'- and marrying the remaining heiress. Times were rough as well as tough. The Macleods thereafter kept firm general control of Lewis for the next two hundred years.

Both 'varieties' of Macleods were sufficiently important for their chiefs to be accounted two out of the four nobles forming the senior level of the Council of the Isles under the Lordship. There were and are, of course, other important families in Lewis of equal or greater antiquity to the Macleods - such as the Morrisons of Ness and the Macaulays of Uig, but they did not expand their territory beyond their immediate spheres of influence after the fall of the Lordship.

The Lewis Macleods were well aware of the importance of the Ui Church. It would, in fact, have been during their hegemony that the bulk of the main sanctuary was built. Tradition tells us that no fewer than 19 of their chiefs were buried at Ui, and not at Iona which might have been expected in that era, though their last resting places at Ui are no longer distinguishable. We know little of their lives though one at least (Torcuil IV) was reckoned to possess every possible chiefly virtue. Unfortunately the last Macleod chief of Lewis (Roderick X), of whom we know most, proved to be a most disreputable rascal with an elastic conscience who fell out most dramatically with the king – which was not very sensible in the late 16th century given that the crown had at long last gained sufficiently in power to do something about their overweening subjects in the uttermost Hebrides. He was then officially deprived of his superiority by the crown.

Mackenzie Stone, artwork by Helen Macdonald

Ui Church   *Simon Riley*

In 1595 Roderick who, notwithstanding the king's displeasure, managed to die at the advanced age of 94 still more or less in the saddle, left a total mess behind him – and certainly that was the case so far as his intended heirs were concerned. He had attempted for rather doubtful reasons to disinherit his legal heir Torcuil (called Conanach - meaning 'of Conon' where he was brought up - to distinguish him from at least four other sons of Roderick also all called Torcuil!) but, unfortunately for his intentions, Torcuil Conanach married into the Mackenzie clan from just across the water in Kintail. Now the Mackenzies and the Macleods had been intertwined for many, many years – for centuries in fact. Their chiefly families had intermarried for a very long time - since at least 1320 - and had been occasionally responsible for each other's executions – formal or informal - since at least 1356.

In any event the Mackenzies of Kintail had probably had their eye on Lewis for ages. When, however, Roderick X fell totally out of favour and had his legal right to the island terminated by King James VI, Kintail saw his chance. He kept his powder dry and when the crown's attempt to colonise Lewis (and incidentally exterminate the populace!) failed, he, as a fellow Gael, was able to bring peace to the island *on behalf of the King* – a small task which the latter had been quite unable to do, and as a result, and in support of his legal claim through Torcuil Conanach, ended up in 1610 with a crown grant of Lewis in his own favour.

The advent of the Mackenzies brought more settled and essentially modern times to Lewis. The Mackenzie chiefs were soon ennobled with the title of 'Seaforth' (after the sea loch of that name on the island's south-east coast). They brought peace and development to the island and an immensely powerful influence UK-wide. The clan's possessions at their height stretched from Lewis right across Scotland to Easter Ross. They became by far the most important and powerful family in the north.

Eastern Chapel, looking west Mike Wood

Eastern Chapel, looking east Mike Wood

Western Chapel Krystyna Pytasz

Some of the Mackenzie clan chiefs spent a good deal of their time in Lewis but only one, William 'Dubh' (the 'black'), the 5th Earl of Seaforth was actually buried at Ui. Many clansmen followed in their wake and their descendants are to be found in considerable numbers on the island even yet. The Seaforth chiefs, after a sticky start with the remnants of the previous Macleod regime, were themselves the last chiefs, properly so called, to rule Lewis and by the time they had run their course were held in great respect by all the islanders save perhaps by a disaffected few.

It is currently thought that the Western Chapel at Ui was added by the Mackenzies, possibly initially as a burial aisle - to put their particular stamp on the site, the importance of which they fully appreciated. Architecturally its style appears more ancient than the main sanctuary but that is not in fact the case. It was not built quite so substantially as was the main sanctuary, but remained in use for a long time after the earlier building was deliberately de-roofed. The church as a whole remained the Parish Church of Stornoway for a very long time - though it could be that some of its functions were unofficially taken over by certain new churches which were built in the then rapidly developing town of Stornoway of the 17th century some three miles distant. That probably remained the situation until 1794 when a new St Columba's Parish Church was built in Stornoway. Thereafter Ui Church would have been reduced to serving the purely local community of the Rubha though its glory days were not forgotten. The great and the good and possibly the not so great or so good of Stornoway continued to be buried in the Ui churchyard as hallowed by the usage of centuries until Sandwick cemetery, more conveniently for the town, was opened in the 1790s.

Detail in Eastern Chapel   Mike Wood

So many interments took place at Ui over many centuries that the ground level rose by several feet all around the old buildings. Originally the graveyard would have been circular, with the church centrally positioned in it, but gradually over the centuries the sea has encroached from the north and now only half of the original area remains intact.

The local Church of Scotland congregation would have continued to worship in the Western Chapel until a new 'Telford' church – now sadly demolished - was built for them just across the road in 1827. It is thought that the chapel remained in occasional use thereafter by the Episcopal Church until 1836 when they built St Peter's in Stornoway for themselves. The chapel remained slate-roofed until 1845/50, but it is thought that the roof may have fallen in round about then.

Grave Stone   Helen Macdonald

Looking west from Ui   Helen Macdonald

The Seaforth line eventually ran out of money and sold the island to (Sir) James Matheson of Hong Kong in 1844. Sir James spent a great deal of his money on improving island roads and such like and introducing industries, but he did not spend much on the Ui Church. Nonetheless he commenced building a never-to-be used mausoleum right next to it - so it is obvious he too appreciated the significance of the site. After the Mathesons came Lord Leverhulme – 1917-23 – who also did not get around to improving matters at Ui. He gifted the whole parish to the people of Stornoway whose interests are now administered by the Stornoway Trust. In turn, in 2012, that Trust gifted the land and buildings at Ui to a specific trust manned by locals concerned with the future of the old church and cemetery – Urras Eaglais na h-Aoidhe. Its remit is to look after what remains to us and where possible to preserve and restore it. Everything was in a pretty bad way until the Urras came on the scene and in just the last few years it has stabilised the walls and has strengthened them so that it may be possible some day, if further and sufficient funding is found, for the building to be re-roofed and restored to community use. So far more than £300,000 has been spent essentially to ensure that the walls do not collapse into the sea – though more has to be done in that connection.

A number of the pre-Reformation (pre-1560) priests are known to us by name (but not much else) from 1426 onwards. Post Reformation ministers are equally scarce until after 1690 when Presbyterianism was permanently established in Scotland – though it took time for much change to percolate through to the isles and squabbles between those who adhered to the new faith and the old religion were not, for a time, uncommon.

Artistic impression of the early church   *David Simon*

When visiting the ancient church be sure to note the way in which the old walls have been capped with turf. That might have been deliberate when the sanctuary was de-roofed and had the effect of preserving the structure and strength of the walls to a very large extent. Had they not been so protected the walls would almost certainly have been reduced to mere rubble over the years. You can see where the rood screen was once fixed and one can see where the priest in charge (who probably lived in the church itself) would have had a fireplace where he could have warmed himself and cooked his food. There are traces of original internal plastering that the gales of the west have not yet managed to remove totally. There would also have been bright lime plaster externally too, but that has all gone. The walls have now been re-pointed and stabilised. A huge amount of concrete had to be poured into a void which had opened up through the action of the tides beneath the floor of the western chapel to make sure that all did not collapse into a heap. Once inside the protective, though temporary, roofing of the Western Chapel, you cannot avoid the splendid memorial stones laid out there, especially that thought to be of Roderick Macleod VII chief of the Siol Thorcuil. Another finely carved slab commemorates his daughter Margaret who died in 1503, she was married to Lachlan Mackinnon and was mother of John, the last Benedictine Abbot of Iona. The more recent 'Mackenzie' stone is not attributed – though the *early* chiefs of that clan tended to carve their Caberfeidh (Stag's head) emblem with a star between the antlers, as is shown on the stone in question. There are also the initials KMK to be found on the edge of the stone and that might well indicate a well-born Kenneth Mackenzie of the early 17th century.

The grounds of the church were for far too long neglected and unkempt, but they are now being regularly mown and it is hoped that it will soon be possible to identify the bulk of the extant memorial stones - especially as a long lost burial record has very recently been traced. Of course, the vast majority of the present extant memorials are of relatively recent 19th century vintage - but work on all that *can* be uncovered will continue - as long as the Urras is supported in that task.

The ultimate long term hope of the Urras is that the buildings may be restored to such an extent that they may be used for weddings and such like romantic occasions, though much of that is unlikely to take place until the Urras' financial well fills up again. Public support is vital and without it nothing at all will happen. There is a Donations Box on site for those who would like to contribute a donation or two. If such a box should have been blown away by the wind or if you have come without an appropriate amount to deposit, why not join the Friends of Ui Church? That can be done via our website at www.uichurch. co.uk where more information about activities and the annual lecture can be obtained. It is hoped that one such will be delivered annually in Lewis by a suitable academic or other well known personage and it is intended that the talks will be gathered together in print and published in due course.

For the moment the place is once more open for all to enjoy - as has not been possible for many a long year and all visitors are welcome to spend as long or as short a time in the precincts as they can afford. Leaflets about Ui Church are available in Bùth an Rubha.

Eilean na Mairbh from Bayble Beach   *Liz Chaplin*

ARCHAEOLOGICAL HIGHLIGHTS OF POINT
Carol Knott

The Outer Hebrides has a very rich heritage of human history since the end of the last Ice Age almost 10,000 years ago, and examples of most of the important features of that history can be found in Point. As the climate slowly warmed, and the bare glaciated rocks became clothed in vegetation, small groups of modern humans appeared in the Islands to hunt the rich resources of the sea and shore, and to gather the fruits of the land. It was not until the arrival of the first farmers, however, almost 6,000 years ago, that mankind began to leave a permanent mark on the landscape. These farming communities of the New Stone Age, or Neolithic Period, cleared the scrubby woodland with stone axes to make fields to graze cattle and sheep, and grew early forms of wheat and barley. (A well preserved axe complete with its wooden shaft was found near Shulishader). Their villages are still quite elusive, but remains of their field systems survive below the present surface, and the sites of their temples, or chambered cairns, still cast a long shadow. Examples of these cairns can be found at Dursainean and Caisteal Mhic Creacail.

Through the following generations a stable farming community became established and Point was well settled with scattered villages and fields. Their monuments included standing stones, of which the best preserved example is Clach Ghlas. Another, Clach Stein (NB 516 317), erected at Lower Bayble, is now fallen and broken, but was the furthest outlier of the main group of stone settings centred on Callanish. From its location the shape of the famous 'Sleeping Beauty' can be seen in the southern hills.

Then there appears to have been a significant change in the climate. Investigations at Sheshader in 1978 have demonstrated presence of original woodland succeeded by grazed grassland followed by the growth of the blanket peat moorland which now covers the interior of Point and gives it its distinctive character, covering over the Neolithic and earlier Bronze Age landscape. The population must have dropped greatly, and the climate became colder and wetter, similar to today.

By about 2,500 years ago, a new Iron Age culture had emerged, based on a pastoral cattle economy. Occupation concentrated around the coast, as now, and the interior was used for rough grazing and fuel. Defended roundhouses became the hallmark of this society, such as the causewayed dun in Loch an Duin, Lower Bayble, or promontory forts such as Dun Dubh, although some of these sites had their origins earlier in prehistory. The Iron Age people of Lewis and Point were undisturbed by the Roman occupation of southern Britain, but from the 5th century AD they found themselves balanced between influences from nearby Ireland, and from the Pictish culture of eastern and northern Scotland.

The arrival of Christianity, however, produced a profound change in the life of Point. Irish and Pictish missionaries came from religious centres such as Iona and Applecross and established a number of cells. One of the most intriguing is the early chapel remains at Tigh an t-Sagairt, Gob na Creige. Most of these foundations, however, survive only as place names. Bayble (Pabail) is a reference to the Papar (priests) who established a monastery somewhere near the mouth of the Bayble river, now lost. The enigmatic site on Eilean na Mairbh may have been used as a hermitage by this community.

Early church traces near Chicken Head *Carol Knott*

Soon this world was disrupted by the arrival of the Vikings, at the end of the 8th century AD. Few Viking remains have yet been found in Point, (notably a soapstone sinker found on a croft in Bayble), but their legacy is clear from the numerous Norse farm and village names throughout the peninsula. The subsequent medieval centuries are attested in stone and mortar at the parish church of Eaglais na h-Aoidhe.

Farming and settlement patterns changed over time, until the arrangement of crofting townships we recognise today was laid out in the later 19th century. Until the 20th century, except for a few churches and school houses, the majority of the population lived in blackhouses. Ruins of some of these remarkable structures can still be seen here and there, but are rapidly disappearing as new houses are built.

Point therefore has a fascinating story to tell of its people, but is one of the least investigated areas of Lewis. There is much more below the surface waiting to be discovered and understood.

1. Clach Ghlas NB 528 334, Garrabost

This dramatic triangular standing stone of local gneiss stands 1.7m tall on a large oval mound 30m long, up to 2m high, the upper part of which is artificial. The stone stands to one side of a rectangular stone-lined depression. A small circular hollow is visible at the NW end of the mound. We do not know the original form and function of this large monument, but the fact that it partly underlies the peat shows that it was perhaps a burial monument of the Neolithic or Bronze Age.

The site is signposted from the main road A866 at Garrabost. Parking is available beside the Free Church. Follow the track for 500m to the SE along the banks of Allt na Muilne (Mill Stream). The site is accessed across the stream by a footbridge.

2. Dursainean NB 523 330, Garrabost

Follow the waymarkers for another 500m to the SW, and you will come to the denuded remains of a Neolithic chambered cairn on top of the hill. Surviving kerbstones indicate that this monument was probably square in plan, with an entrance facing the south-east where the midwinter sun could be observed rising from the mountains of mainland Scotland across the Minch. It would have served as a tribal temple and tomb. For a circular walk you can follow the waymarkers downhill to Graham Avenue.

3. Caisteal Mhic Creacail NB 543 366, Flesherin

Today this cairn is dilapidated and robbed out. At first sight it is hard to imagine that its scattered stones are the remains of another great chambered tomb where the people of this part of Point celebrated their rituals and interred their ancestors. But look carefully and you will see the edge stones of the entrance passage, also aligned to midwinter sunrise.

The cairn lies on the shoreline by a small rocky inlet about 600m to the WNW from the Flesherin road end, across moorland with extensive peat cuttings.

4. Loch an Dùin NB 516 304, Lower Bayble

Built within this loch, near its NE shore, was a small circular dun, connected to the shore by a 22m-long stone causeway, now mostly submerged. This would have been a

Clach Ghlas, Garrabost

Judy Macdonald

defended farmhouse, the residence of one of the principal families of the area. Like all of the sites listed here it has not been archaeologically investigated, but elsewhere island duns like this have sometimes been shown to date to the period 500 BC – 500 AD, although potentially with much earlier origins. Traces of its circular outer stone wall can be seen around its 20m wide perimeter, but there is also the remains of a rectangular building which suggests that it was again used in the later medieval period. The dun may have been built on a natural islet, or it may be a completely man-made construction.

The loch is accessible from a track leading from the Lower Bayble road, but the causeway is not passable. The site of another island dun can be found at Loch an Dùin, Aird, NB 556 359.

5. 'Tigh an t-Sagairt' (House of the priest) NB 507 292, Chicken Head

Low foundations of a small stone-built early medieval chapel. The site is undated, but decorated pottery has been found nearby which may date to around the 10th century AD. It stood in a walled rectangular enclosure, bounded on the north by a rock outcrop. The west side of the enclosure has been remodelled with the insertion of a two-chambered cellular building, and the addition of a number of other structures and a field system.

The chapel remains lie in a lovely spot on the coast where a stream from Loch Cuilc flows over the edge of a cliff. It is best accessed from Swordale, where a peat track leads to a quarry, then a walk of 1200m over the moor south-eastwards to the site. Care is necessary on the cliff-top approach to the site.

6. Eilean na Mairbh NB 535 311, Upper Bayble

This steep sea stack is not accessible, but can be viewed clearly from the adjacent shore only a few metres away. Intriguingly, 'Eilean na Mairbh' translates as 'Island of the Dead'.

Substantial stone walling can be seen along the northern, landward edge of the stack. On the narrow summit are low grassed-over remains of at least one stone structure and midden deposits containing animal bones, shells and pottery, indicating that someone was living and eating meals there for some length of time, possibly about 1000 years ago. There is no evidence at present, however, of any graves.

Eilean na Mairbh is visible from Bayble pier looking east. For a closer look, take the track around the marina, then follow the coastline for 750m, taking care on cliff-tops.

7. Dun Dubh promontory fort, NB 557 326, Sheshader

The promontory of Dun Dubh is defended by a well-built stone wall, 4.5m thick, across the narrow neck of land connecting it to Point, with a narrow entrance in the centre. Its outer face is clearly visible but the inner face is almost covered by silt from the sloping interior of the fort. The rest of the perimeter is protected by steep cliffs. The fort is undated, but may have been used by Iron Age people, possibly as a safe refuge for cattle, and there may once have been huts and other buildings inside the fort.

Dun Dubh can be reached from the Sheshader road end and following the coast for about 1km. Remains of another promontory fort can be found at Dùn Mòr, Garrabost (NB 513 339).

Garrabost shoreline   *Christeen Mackenzie*

NATURAL HISTORY OF POINT
Mark Macdonald

Point has a number of advantages which have long rendered it one of the most popular parts of Lewis for those interested in the beauty and variety of creation. It is within easy reach of Stornoway, it shares with other areas around Stornoway a geology distinct from most of the rest of Lewis, and its best spots for seeing wildlife are easily accessible from the road – often without even having to leave the car!

A wildlife tour of Point always begins at the Braighe. Both Loch Branahuie and the sea south of the sea-wall are easily observed from the car using one of the lay-bys along the main road. The loch and adjoining machair often attract rare migratory birds, especially in spring and autumn, but their main interest lies in more regular species. The machair is a result of a build up of calcium rich shell sand being blown over the land and enriching the soil. In high summer the machair supports a wide range of colourful flowers such as buttercup, red clover, eyebright, yellow rattle, selfheal, wild thyme and silverweed. Thrift is particularly colourful along the Braighe Road.

In the spring, long-tailed ducks which have spent the winter on the surrounding sea congregate in increasing numbers on Loch Branahuie in the build-up to migration, when the males' long tail feathers and whistling call are unmistakeable. Greylag geese are also present in large numbers, either grazing on the turf or loafing on the water. Aggressive encounters between individuals can often be seen as they prepare to pair off and disperse to the surrounding moorland to breed. Curlews are ever-present in winter and lapwing

From the top Curlew, Lapwing, Oyster Catchers and Ringed Plovers   Virtual Hebrides

flocks move between here and the fields towards Stornoway.

On the sea, striking male red-breasted mergansers and the more dowdy females dive for fish close to the shore, while further out other diver species can be spotted with a little patience. In May black-throated divers gather in groups of up to a dozen, looking especially sleek in their newly-acquired breeding plumage of chequered back, velvety-grey nape and black and white neck. In their more subdued winter plumage, they can be distinguished from the similar but larger great northern diver by their white patch near the 'stern', just above the water line.

From May to August the Braighe is usually busy with Arctic terns from the large colony at Melbost. They hover above the water before making an elegant plunge-dive for a sandeel. One or two little terns can usually be detected among the many Arctics. They can be distinguished by their shorter tails, white foreheads and especially much faster wing beats. They are usually found nearer the Point end of the beach.

The first village over the Braighe is Aignish. The little beach (Aignish Beach) on the Broad Bay side is well worth a visit. Reach it by taking the first left after the Braighe and proceeding to the end of this road, where you may park before reaching a field gate. If the tide is out, this is a great place to watch common (or harbour) seals hauled out on the skerries just out from the shore. There can be 20-30 seals here at times. These are smaller than the grey seals which can sometimes be seen bobbing in the water at the Braighe, the latter also distinguishable by their 'Roman nose' profile.

This beach is especially good in spring and autumn for passage waders, which use it as a staging post between their breeding grounds in the Arctic and wintering quarters further south. Sanderling, knot and black- and bar-tailed godwits are often here as well as the more common curlew, oystercatcher, dunlin and turnstone.

Back on the main road, the shore at the end of the Rathad na Ceardaich can produce sightings of otter for anyone with the patience to sit quietly and wait. However, this is by no means guaranteed! Otters are present all around the coast of Point, except the high cliff sections, but seeing one (which often leads to seeing a few more, if it's a family group) is about being in the right place at the right time. They sometimes follow streams inland, either to hunt eels and frogs, or to drink and wash in freshwater, but are usually easier to spot on the sea shore, if you can identify their dark wet backs amongst the rocks and seaweed.

Otters are sometimes confused with mink, as they are both brown, semi-aquatic members of the weasel family. American mink have been a pest in Lewis and Harris for over 50 years since they escaped (or were released) from failing fur farms and became established in the wild. Point has been a hotspot for them, to the extent that keeping poultry became almost impossible at some locations. The Hebridean Mink Project has been engaged for some years in a large-scale, systematic trapping programme aimed at eradicating this species, which has considerable impacts on wild birds in addition to fisheries and poultry. This project has been very successful, to the extent that at the time of writing, there are thought to be very few of these predators remaining in Lewis and Harris. Mink are smaller, thinner, and darker than otters. They are blackish brown all over with a short, thin tail (otter tails are long and thick) and white lower lip

Sanderling and Arctic Tern   *Virtual Hebrides*

Greylag Geese and Starling   *Simon Riley*

From the top Dunlin, Gannet, Arctic Skua, Common Terns   Virtual Hebrides

and chin. Any sightings, or other evidence of mink, should be reported as soon as possible.

Between Aignish and Garrabost the rocky shoreline rises to low cliffs. Close inspection shows that the rock here is quite different to the Lewisian gneiss which makes up most of the island. It is a sedimentary conglomerate, known as the Stornoway Beds, which extends from the town to the southern half of Broad Bay, about as far as Garrabost on the east side and Gress on the west. It has the appearance of pebbles set in concrete. The difference is especially striking at a point below Garrabost where the gneiss and the conglomerate abut against each other, though this spot is a little hard to get to. Sea campion can be found on the rocky cliffs, with yellow primroses on the grass above and, where salt spray splashes the rocks, sea plantain and thrift can be seen.

Unlike the metamorphic cliffs on the Minch side of the peninsula, the conglomerate has few ledges suitable for seabirds to nest on. Fulmars find an odd pocket, as do ravens, whose inaccessible large nests of dead heather and debris are not difficult to locate. The caves are used by rock doves, where they construct nests as flimsy as the ravens' are substantial. These doves are the favourite prey of the peregrine, our largest breeding falcon, which is also sometimes seen along this stretch of coast.

The corncrake can be heard calling from crofts almost anywhere in Point, but is most reliable in Aignish and Garrabost. They may fly to and from Africa every year, but they are very reluctant to take to the wing once they arrive here in early May, and even more loathe to stray far from thick vegetation. When they first arrive the only long vegetation tends to be around wetter area such as ditches or marshy ground with iris, and this is where they are usually first heard. The male's distinctive call, "stiff card on comb next to a megaphone", is the source of its scientific name, Crex crex. Later in the season, they move out into long grass such as on crofts which are grown for hay and silage.

To the south-east of the main road are two extensive areas of peaty moorland containing blanket bog habitat, one between Knock and Lower Bayble, and a larger area between Garrabost, Upper Bayble, Sheshader and Shulishader. These are home to a good mix of moorland and coastal breeding birds in summer, but are almost empty in winter. The moorland is covered by peat, a dark fibrous type of soil derived from dead plant material. If rainfall is higher than water loss through drainage and evaporation the soil becomes permanently waterlogged. Soil acidity rises and the dead vegetation does not rot completely. Bell heather, cross-leaved heath and heather or ling are common species on the moorland. Plants such as heath spotted orchid, bog asphodel, the small yellow flowered tormentil, blue, purple or pink heath milkwort, as well as the insectivorous sundew and butterwort are commonly found here. There are also expanses of white cotton-grass and various mosses, rushes and sedges.

Probably the most obvious birds on the moor in summer are the two skua species. Although these are true seabirds which spend much of the year in the Atlantic, they nest in loose colonies on the ground on coastal moorland. The Arctic skua is the smaller and more graceful of the two. It is dark brown above with long pointed wings, elongated central tail feathers and a characteristic "miaowing" call. There are two colour phases, one dark all over, the other with a creamy white breast and

Thrift and Birdsfoot Trefoil　　　　　*Simon Riley*

Flag Iris and Wild Thyme　　　　　*Virtual Hebrides*

Ragged Robin   *Janet Cameron*

Thistles   *Judy Macdonald*

Ling   *Virtual Hebrides*

Cotton Grass   *Judy Macdonald*

belly. The great skua or bonxie is bigger and bulkier, dark mottled brown all over with distinctive white flashes in the wings in flight. Both species obtain much of their food by stealing fish from other seabirds. Arctic skuas can frequently be seen chasing terns at the Braighe in pursuit of their catch of sandeels, when their speed and aerobatic ability is most impressive. Bonxies also frequently kill other birds, including the young of their smaller relatives. This might explain the relative change in numbers of the two species – 30 years ago Arctic skuas were much more numerous in Point, but now the situation is reversed.

Another distinctive behaviour of skuas is their aggressive defence of their nests, especially after the eggs have hatched. Many a Rubhach peat-cutter has set out for a day at the peats complete with hard hat and stick, or even a crash helmet! The skuas vigorously dive-bomb anyone straying too close to the nest – moving quickly away soon calms them down.

Red-throated divers nest on a few small lochans on the moor, and commute to the sea to fish, where their goose-like cackling is often heard, especially on a still evening. Another distinctive sound of dusk in spring and early summer is the drumming of snipe. As the males fly steeply downwards, stiff outer tail feathers vibrate against the airflow, giving a unique sound from moor and marsh. Marshy areas are often rich in plant species with marsh marigold, lady's smock or cuckoo flower, ragged robin, yellow iris and northern marsh orchid being commonly found.

The golden plover or feadag often accompanies the moor walker, keeping a wary eye on him as it gives its sad whistle, runs a few steps, then stops to look and whistle once more. It is often attended by its smaller relative the dunlin, identified by its slightly curved bill, black belly and characteristic trilling call.

The red grouse, locally known as moorhen, is widespread in Lewis but infrequent in Point. The same goes for its main predator the golden eagle, with just the occasional wandering immature bird being seen. There are a few pairs of our smallest bird of prey, the merlin, which nests in thick heather and speeds over the moor, skimming the vegetation, hunting skylarks and meadow pipits. The song of the skylark, from high above croft and moor, is one of the defining sounds of mid-summer. The meadow pipit seems like a cheap imitation – similar looking but smaller, it also sings in the air while parachuting to the ground. But it only gets a few metres off the ground, and its song of repeated peep-peep-peeps has none of the variety of the lark.

Further into Point there are two roadside lochs which are always worth checking for birds. Loch an Duin at Aird hosts one of the largest Arctic tern colonies in the Hebrides in summer, which has thrived with the progress of mink eradication. Loch an Tiumpan, by the minor road to the lighthouse, has a number of lay-bys convenient for birdwatching. It has a resident population of tufted duck, mallard and teal, as well as feral ducks. In winter wildfowl numbers are swelled by wigeon and whooper swan as well as occasional rarer species like scaup and American wigeon.

Tiumpan Head itself is an excellent vantage point to watch marine wildlife from, as well as affording exceptional views of the mainland. But great care should always be taken, especially to the west of the lighthouse, where the grassy slopes above the cliffs can be treacherously slippery.

Otter and Seals *Virtual Hebrides*

Seal at Aignish Beach *Simon Riley*

This is arguably the best land-based vantage point for observing cetaceans (whales and dolphins) in the whole of the UK. The relatively slow-moving Risso's dolphins are often quite close to shore, and can be identified by their light grey colouration, blunt head and large dorsal fin. Minke whales often feed close in as well, in the turbulent water to the north of the lighthouse. White-beaked dolphins are a stocky species with light and dark markings on their back and flanks, and tend to be only viewed at distance as they stay a bit further offshore. The harbour porpoise is our smallest cetacean species and very common, though often difficult to spot as they roll over unobtrusively at the surface showing a dark back and low, triangular fin. A calm day in summer and autumn is best for all these species, as well as for basking sharks. Our largest shark species can be identified as both the dorsal fin and the tip of the tail wave above the surface as it cruises around for plankton in the sunlit upper layers of the sea. Basking sharks seem to be becoming more numerous as their numbers slowly recover from the hunting which carried on until a few decades ago.

The cliffs at Tiumpan Head hold seabirds such as kittiwake, guillemot, razorbill, fulmar, shag and great black-backed gull. In fact groups of these species can be found on the cliffs along most of the south-east side of the peninsula, from Sheshader to Bayble and round to Swordale. Gannets are always passing by in summer, and can often be watched as they circle high above a shoal of mackerel or sandeels before making their spectacular dive to catch one beneath the waves. Pairs of ravens are also spread along this coast. In winter the small, black and white barnacle goose can sometimes be found feeding on short clifftop grass here or on Bayble Island.

The above account is aimed at giving a taster of what can be seen. No doubt much has been omitted that others can find for themselves. Hopefully these few pointers will give some idea of the potential of this favoured part of Lewis.

Cotton Grass   *Janet Cameron*

Aerial view of the western end of Point showing pattern of crofts   *Chris Murray*

CROFTING
Angus Macdonald

You would have to be born into crofting to have any hope of understanding it and even then it can defy definition. It involves working small units of land, which can vary in size from a few acres, to areas resembling small farms in some parts of the Highlands and Islands. In the Point district, crofts are generally small. The land gives enough space for a family home, and the agricultural activity can vary from planting crops and grazing for livestock, to crofts where today, no cultivation takes place. Crofts generally stretch out on either side of the road through each village. Each is defined by the fences marking the croft boundaries which have remained more or less the same since the 19th century.

What is indisputable, however, is that crofting itself has changed. Following decades of starvation for the population of the Highlands and Islands through having too little land, the threat of being cleared from the land to make way for something more profitable, and widespread agitation against rapacious landowners, the 1886 Crofters Act gave crofters security of tenure - without giving them enough land on which to live. That led to more unrest throughout the Highlands and Islands as destitute crofters sought to take back land that they felt had been stolen from their ancestors by the landowners.

In the Point area, desperation led the people to try to seize the farm at Aignish in what became known as the Aignish Riot on Monday 9th January 1888. 13 men were arrested and jailed, but it would take until the early years of the 20th century before the crofting village was finally established. From the end of the 18th century, there were periods of people being forcibly removed from their land, and landowners often made them emigrate to Canada, the United States and some ended up in Australia. Even at the beginning of the 20th century, poverty and lack of opportunity saw large numbers of people moving out of the Western Isles. Some moved to the mainland. People from Point found a new home in Skye where they settled with other crofters from Lewis and Harris. Others were part of the mass emigrations to Canada which began in 1923.

Today Aignish is the first village to meet the visitor to Point after crossing the isthmus known as the Braighe (Am Bràighe). Just at the Point end of the Braighe, on the left-hand side is a monument erected to commemorate the part Aignish played in the land struggle. It was always the most fertile area of Point with its sandy, well-drained soil, but like other villages, the crofts are not as intensively cultivated now as they once were.

Surviving on very little has been the characteristic of crofting for centuries. Crofting changed from a system where crofts were re-lotted every few years, to ensure no one was stuck with unproductive land, to assigning each family their own croft on a long-term basis. For many, that involved double-digging several acres with a spade. This involved removing the turf, digging down to twice the depth of the spade, putting the turf face-down in the bottom of the trench and covering that with soil. It also involved working in animal manure and seaweed, and sometimes sand where the soil was excessively peaty. Large families were common and the women carried a huge share of the work burden. This was particularly true if the crofter was also a fisherman, which could mean months away from home as the fleet followed the herring shoals around the British coast.

The food produced on the croft, combined with the dairy products supplied by one or two cows, and meat from cattle and sheep was supplemented by fish and shellfish, with peat providing fuel. Board of Agriculture loans and grants helped to replace the thatched houses with more substantial buildings, although most rural areas in Lewis had to wait until the 1950s for electricity and water. Even though crofters often had other employment, such as fishing, weaving, mill-work, construction, or hiring themselves out for croft work, it was in the main an almost subsistence economy until after the Second World War.

Crofting still contributed significantly to the household income until well into the 1980s. The year started with the spring lambing and planting of the crops. The sheep were kept on the croft or on the common grazing land behind the villages. The sheep were fed daily to support them into the spring until the grass started growing and they had to be checked from dawn till nightfall, and sometimes they had to be nursed through the night. Horses gave way to tractors for the agricultural work, and potato planting, hay-making and the corn harvest and threshing of the grain, were all communal activities. Potatoes were planted not only for the household but also to be used as part of the feeding for livestock throughout the winter. Oats and barley were the two main grain crops that were planted. Hens were common and they also had to be fed, and the byre and henhouse mucked out regularly.

Cutting peats also required the help of neighbours, unless the family was large enough to crew the work themselves. With open fires then the only means of heating houses, most households needed seven or eight tractor trailer loads to see them through the year. First came the turfing, to remove the heather and top layer of soil to reach the peat itself. Then the crews, two people at a time, started cutting with the tairsgeir, specially designed to make slabs that were thrown on the top of the peat bank to dry. The deeper the peat bank, and some of them were six peats deep, the further the peats had to be thrown. A few weeks later, after hardening slightly, the peats would then be lifted to allow the wind to get through them. After further shifting, and drying, they would be gathered and taken home.

The sheep and cattle were taken to summer pasture on the moorland area west and south of Stornoway, from the Barvas road, over to the Barvas hills and as far south as Achmore, to rest the crofts and to give the potatoes and other crops a chance to grow. Point is unique in that each village has been allocated grazings on the moor, many miles away from the villages in the district. This was because the Point area was thought to have too little grazing area of its own and each village in Point was assigned its own common grazing area on the moor.

Crofting in Point   Simon Riley

In previous decades families used to decamp from most of the villages in Lewis, with their livestock, to spend most of the summer in sheilings, or àirighean, on the moor. This transhumance is mirrored in many other European countries, and is a feature of pastoral societies whose existence is dependent on their flocks and herds. What made it different for the Point area was the distance people had to travel to get

Crofts in Knock, early 1980s   Christeen Mackenzie

to their own area of the moor. Most of the other villages throughout the island just had to travel into the moor behind their villages. The remains of the original àirigh buildings, built of stone, just like the black houses, can still be seen in many areas of the moor. The practice of going to the àirigh continues to the present day, where some people use the àirigh for a summer holiday, although the sheilings now are built of corrugated iron, or even concrete blocks.

Hay was cut from July onwards depending on the growth, and it then had to be dried and stacked to feed sheep and cows through the winter. In the present day most of the work is done by tractors and balers, and the vagaries of the weather can be overcome by making silage bales. Oats were cut later and there were times when some of the work would be done under the harvest moon. Potatoes were lifted during the school 'potato holidays' in October and taken into the byre for winter storage. Sometimes the potatoes and other vegetables were lifted and dug into a 'sloc' - a pit in the ground where the vegetables were covered in straw and then soil was heaped on top, and they were dug up as they were required.

Meat and fish were also part of the diet. Sheep were slaughtered on the croft with most parts of the animal being put to some use. Before the advent of fridges, the meat would be salted and kept dark and cool, usually in the byre, to preserve it as long as possible. Most households would have a barrel or two of salt herring, and whitefish, such as cod, ling and eel would also be available. The strange thing was that in the days before the ro-ro ferries, the mailboat could be off for days and few people would notice. They had plenty of food set aside to see them through - a far cry from the panic-buying in the Stornoway supermarkets when the ferry is cancelled now.

Many of the crofts will still be used for hay since in most villages there are a number of active crofters who make use of crofts where neighbours might have grown too old for croft work, or where they might have decided that the returns no longer justify the effort. The cultivation of potatoes, oats, barley and vegetables such as turnips, carrots, cabbage, beetroot and onions has also declined as growing commitment to other types of employment has reduced the available time, and Stornoway supermarkets have held out the temptation of convenience. Livestock numbers have also declined and while sheep are still common in most villages, cattle numbers have dropped disastrously. Cattle are excellent for grazing rough pasture and old grass, encouraging new growth which benefits both cattle and sheep.

Crofting is a regulated system. Many of the crofts are rented from the Stornoway Trust, the first community landowner, which was established in 1923. Members of the Trust are elected periodically by the residents of the Stornoway parish which covers from Tolsta in the north, the villages around Stornoway, Stornoway itself, Point and down to the border with North Lochs, south of Stornoway. Crofters in Point are, therefore, in the interesting position that they rent land from themselves, but this does not mean that they can escape the duties placed on all crofters by the Crofting Commission.

Crofters must live on, or very near, their crofts. They must work their crofts, although the type of work is defined very widely, and there are strict rules about who can succeed them as croft tenants. Usually this is a family member, but again they must live on the croft and work it. Other crofters in a village can also object to any proposed new tenant whom they feel to be unsuitable. Crofts also come under the supervision of grazings committees, which are usually chosen from among the crofters in each village. The committees also regulate the 'common grazings' which are the areas outwith the crofts, and in Point this is the rough heathery ground behind the villages. The common grazing is used to feed the livestock and to relieve the pressure on the crofts and are also still used by some for peat-cutting.

Things have changed and where once all the crofts were worked, it is now more common to see several crofts being worked by the one crofter. Another common element is that active crofters tend to be retirees or offshore workers. The issues of time and available finance are important factors in an activity that once provided a significant supplement to the household income - now it generally costs more than it earns in income.

Some of the crofts have been used for house sites for succeeding generations and it is common to see some crofts with two or three houses. Some appear to have been given over to housing, although this is now frowned on by the Crofting Commission.

Why would you persist with a form of agriculture that costs more than you earn from it? Why would you try to produce something from land which resists you at every turn? Why would you care for a type of livestock whose dominant trait is causing frustration through not growing consistently, damaging fencing or simply dropping dead? Because it is in the blood.

Peat Stack, Garrabost, early 1980s   *Christeen Mackenzie*

1937 Photograph of the Muirneag at Stornoway on transit to or from ling fishing at St. Kilda.
Donald Mackay

THE FISHING
Alex John Murray

History

The fishing industry has been of tremendous importance to the people of the island of Lewis for hundreds of years, as it has been the main source of employment and income for many. Point, along with the districts of Lochs, Back and Tolsta, provided more fishermen in the days of herring drift net fishing and sail than any other part of the island. In 1898 there were forty one first class fishing boats registered at Stornoway of between 30' and 70' keel length, owned and crewed by fishermen from the district of Point; each boat carried a crew of seven to nine men.

All of these boats would have taken part in the North Minch herring fishing, landing their catches into Stornoway, Gairloch, Ullapool and Lochinver, with eight or nine of the smaller boats turning to the inshore whitefish long line fishing during the winter months. Their catch consisted mainly of cod, haddock, ling, conger eel, skate and plaice. There was also a large number of small open boats ranging in overall length from 12' to the 25' *'sgoth'* in all the villages in Point fishing with wooden home-made creels mainly for lobsters, and hand-lines for lythe, haddock, ling and saithe, and selling their catches in their local villages. On returning from the fishing grounds most of these small boats had to be hauled up on the beach above the high water mark, this practice continued into the late 1950s.

In the latter years of the 19th and early 20th centuries Point produced many notable seamen and fishermen; one being Alexander Macleod skipper/owner of possibly the most famous of all the fishing boats in the Western Isles - *Muirneag SY486*. In 1886, at the age of nineteen, Macleod ordered a new *'sgoth'* type fishing boat called the *Jubilee* from Stornoway boat-builder Murdo Macdonald. Although he fished her for the next four years he found that because of her size he was restricted in which fishing grounds he could go to, so in 1890 he sold the *Jubilee* and as skipper and part-owner, took over another Zulu type, the 49' keel *Johanna SY853*.

In the *Johanna* Macleod experienced one of his worst trips to sea. After leaving Loch Inchard south of Cape Wrath at 8am one December morning in 1891, with 120 cran of herring on board bound for Stornoway, it blew a full gale from the southwest; they had to shorten sail to the last reef at 10am. He was still at the wheel when, at 11pm that night, still on the port tack, they made landfall at the Butt of Lewis. Shortly after coming about to the starboard tack the foreyard broke and the sail was torn. They got the mizzen sail rigged up on the foremast, but after some time the yard broke and the sail was damaged. While lying helplessly

Image from the glass slide lantern collection of Bob Davis, Taunton, Somerset

broadside on, a heavy sea struck and almost swamped her. They then rigged up and streamed a sea anchor to bring her head to the sea and rode it out until 10am the following morning when the wind moderated and shifted westerly. They then spliced the yard with wooden fend-offs, patched up the sail as best they could and slowly made their way to Lochinver, approximately 30 miles south of Loch Inchard, arriving at 4pm that day. The only other boat caught in the gale disappeared without trace.

Six years later in 1896 the *Jubilee* was sold and Macleod became skipper and part-owner of another Zulu type the 54' keel fishing boat the *Caberfeigh SY 1108*, which was built to his own specification. This was the first Stornoway fishing boat to fish the East Anglian winter herring fishing.

In 1898 they sold the *Caberfeigh* and purchased the eight month old 60' keel fishing boat *Morven SY1217* from Wick. One morning, after hauling 50 cran of herring in the North Minch in a south westerly gale and making for Stornoway, the Macbrayne's passenger ship

RMS *Clansman* came up with them. The *Morven* with two reefs in the sail and running before a heavy sea was in Stornoway at the same time as the *Clansman*. Another stormy night the RMS *Claymore,* another of Macbrayne's passenger ships, was storm bound at Kyle of Lochalsh. Macleod took the *Morven* alongside the *Claymore* and offered to take the mails across to Stornoway for them before crossing the Minch that night.

One winter, on the home passage from Lowestoft, the *Morven* arrived at Stornoway fourteen days ahead of the other Stornoway boats, which had accompanied her all the way north to Wick. Encountering heavy weather from the north, the other boats put into Wick, but Macleod kept the *Morven* going into the Pentland Firth, where they had to reef down to two reefs in the foresail and four in the mizzen sail. He was at the wheel all night without being relieved. With the *Morven,* Alexander Macleod was the first skipper from the Western Isles to fish out of Lowestoft.

In 1903 Macleod contacted William MacIntosh, a renowned boatbuilder in Portessie Buckie, and ordered an 80' Zulu type fishing boat with certain amendments to suit his own requirements derived from his experience on the Zulu type boats. With two such experienced men combined, one the master boat-builder craftsman, the other the master skipper and seaman, the result could not but produce a masterpiece and the *Muirneag SY486,* as he named her, was all of that. The *Muirneag* under full sail was a good, safe, powerful sea boat which hardly ever needed to be eased in a heavy sea.

Macleod was a hard driver. He drove all his boats relentlessly, especially the *Muirneag,* which could stand being hard pressed. As he once said himself "I never worry about the *Muirneag's hull, only the spars and gear"* and many of these were broken. Macleod refused to convert the *Muirneag* to motor power, he preferred sail. She was the last of the sail boats of that size in Britain still wholly depending on sail. When sold to be broken up in 1947 the *Muirneag* had never changed ownership, Macleod was the sole owner and skipper for the exceptionally long period of 42 years.

It is indeed ironic that more than 100 years after Alexander Macleod became the first Stornoway skipper to take his fishing boat to the East Anglian fishing grounds, his great grandson Alexander Murdo Murray should sail out of Stornoway in his 68' motor powered fishing boat the *Astra SY153* to fish the same East Anglian grounds.

Both the first and second World Wars took their toll on the fishing industry with the loss of so many young men that the number of registered fishing boats operating out of Stornoway from the Point area was down to 9 by 1930 and by 1956/57 only the 65' *Golden Sheaf* SY229 and the 55' *Renown* SY14 were left. By 1961 both of these Point owned boats brought the herring drift net fishing in the Western Isles to an end, when they were converted to a new type of fishing, trawling for nephrops and whitefish.

Shipping Accidents

Although there were many fishing boats wrecked on the Point coast as well as drownings the following spring to mind more than others.

In September 1923, about 2.5 miles from Stornoway Harbour, the RMS passenger ship *Sheila* was proceeding south towards Kyle of Lochalsh when she was in collision with the

Stornoway registered motor fishing boat *Violas,* which was owned and crewed by Point fishermen. The *Violas,* which was lying on the end of a fleet of herring drift nets in thick fog, was cut 'into' between midships and bow on the port side, she sank in six to eight minutes with the loss of one of her crew. As soon as the *Sheila* backed off the *Violas* filled with water and rapidly began to sink. The crew rushed to launch the small boat, but only four of them were able to get on board before the painter snapped and the small boat started to drift away from the *Violas.* With the small boat drifting away in thick

Muirneag, image from family sources

fog, the men on board were unable to row back and rescue the remaining three crewmen; at the same time one of the *Sheila's* small boats was launched, but only two of the remaining three crewmen were found swimming about in the sea. The *Sheila* put back to Stornoway with the two that were plucked from the sea, while the four on the small boat beached on the east side of No. 1 pier in Stornoway.

A tragedy occurred at Bayble on the morning of Tuesday 4th October 1938. On a stormy night, with the wind blowing a full gale from the NW, two steam trawlers were sheltering in Bayble Bay. The Grimsby registered *Carrisbrook* was anchored off the north end of Bayble Island when five young men, aged between 15 and 21, from Upper Bayble decided to launch one of the small boats from the beach and row out to her. As the small boat approached the *Carrisbrook* the short lumpy seas were splashing heavily over the bow; one of them managed to climb on to the *Carrisbrook* deck and secured the painter from the small boat, then the other four were able to join him on board.

As the sea swell increased they asked the trawler skipper to tow the small boat closer inshore to more sheltered water. The skipper refused, and angrily told them to get back in the small boat, which they refused to do. After a further angry exchange of words, the skipper agreed to their request *'on condition they got into the small boat before he would tow them'.* As the 15 year old sole survivor said afterwards: "Up until this point we had felt safe. Once back in the small boat, under tow, disaster was inevitable in such conditions. The tow was too fast, the tow rope too short, the wash from the propeller worsened the yawing, coming sharply out of a yaw to starboard the sideways pull on the tow made the bow dip just as a wave approached. It poured noisily over the bow. Almost in a flash we were all in a maelstrom of foaming water". That was the last he saw of his four friends. The tow rope broke and the momentum took the boat down deep. He struggled to the surface; though shaken and having some difficulty staying afloat at first, he became aware of his surroundings, night was falling and he could see the lights of the *Carrisbrook* some distance away. He swam around aimlessly, sometimes just treading water, then in the fading light he saw the unmistakeable shape of the upturned boat on the top of a wave and disappearing briefly into the trough. Fully clothed he managed to undo his bootlaces and prise each boot off in turn; he then began to swim towards the upturned boat. Holding on to the rubbing strake while trying to climb on

Muirneag on her way to be broken up, image credited to Roddy Macdonald

to the top, the boat rolled over towards him and righted itself, though fully submerged. He got onboard and by sitting in the middle it was buoyant enough to hold his weight. The water was up to his waist and he was almost numb with the cold.

The wind had dropped and the sea was considerably calmer; he could see by her lights that the *Carrisbrook* was coming about and heading towards him; as they came in close a searchlight was shone at him and after some difficulty the crew were able to take him on board. The moment of truth for him was when he was taken down to the crew quarters - there was no one else there, he was on his own. To avoid immediate arrest the skipper steamed the *Carrisbrook* three miles out from the nearest point of land, before calling the lifeboat, which took the sole survivor to Stornoway. Later at the High Court in Edinburgh, the skipper of the *Carrisbrook* was found guilty of having been responsible for the death of four young men by drowning and sentenced to 8 months imprisonment.

In December 1953, the same night as the car ferry *Princess Victoria* sank in the North Channel while on passage from Stranraer to Larne, the 80' Zulu type boat *Delight SY186,* skippered and crewed by Point fishermen, put to sea. They shot their drift nets on a calm evening two miles SW of Tiumpan Head and hauled a shot of approximately 60 cran of herring three miles off Bayble in the early hours of the following morning. While the skipper set course for Ullapool, the crew set about clearing the deck, cleaning and stacking the nets. Suddenly the wind backed into the north and blew a full gale. The *Delight* was built for sail, but had been converted to engine power. Before the crew got all the nets stacked in the open fish hold, a heavy sea struck the boat midships and the sea burst the for'ard bulkhead in the hold as well as washing the mizzen mast and sail overboard along with some of the nets which fouled the propeller. With the engines out of commission, the boat drifted with the wind and in an attempt to bring her "head to sea" the crew paid out the remaining nets, but the wind was so severe that their action had no effect, and in pitch darkness the boat drifted helplessly across the Minch.

During daylight the momentum carried her clear of Priest Island at the southern entrance to Loch Broom towards the rocks at Gruinard Bay; noticing a sandy beach west of the rocks, they rigged a small sail on the foremast, this carried her clear of the rocks and she drifted towards the sandy beach. As the boat slowly approached the sandy beach, the crew tied two drift net buoys together for holding on to in the hope that when the boat grounded on the long shallow beach the buoys would carry them ashore. The small boat was launched with five crewmen as soon as the boat grounded, but was swamped by the huge sea running towards the beach; by holding on to the buoys the sea carried the men ashore. Their plan worked and the remaining three were saved by the same method. They were taken to the Loch Ewe naval base for the night. They returned to the scene the following morning, only to find pieces of the boat scattered across the beach, and the two engines half buried in the sand.

Recent Times

By 1959/60 new types of fishing were being practiced by Point fishermen, namely trawl fishing for nephrops and whitefish as well as a pair trawling for herring and mackerel. The nephrop (variously called Norway lobster, Dublin Bay prawn or langoustine) was the most successful and lucrative fishing to take place since the late 1940s. Again as with the earlier herring fishing, the fishing grounds off the Bayble coast proved to be the most productive in the North Minch. By the mid 1970s the number of boats in the 30' to 70' class part-owned by Point fishermen had increased to 11. In 2013 there was only one boat of that class owned and fished by a Point fisherman, the *Astra SY153*.

The decline in the number of fishing boats is mainly down to European Union legislation which prohibits fishermen from fishing to their full capacity because of a quota on the amount of fish and shellfish they are allowed to catch, as well as a restriction on the number of days they can fish in a given year; this has made the industry uneconomical for most fishermen and forced them to abandon fishing; in most cases selling their boats for scrap value.

The fishing grounds adjacent to the Point coast were as rich in species as any fishing grounds in the UK; landmarks such as Tiumpan Head, Black Sandy (Dun Dubh), Bible Head (Bayble Head), Old Adam (Eilean na Crotach) and Chicken Rock were as familiar to herring fishermen from around the UK as they were to locals.

Images of the Muirneag sourced from http://glennmci.brinkster.net/mng/mng.html

Bayble Beach   Janet Cameron

Point – An Rubha

Most of the placenames in Point or An Rubha are derived
from Gaelic or Norse and sometimes a mixture of both.
For example, the village of Knock has its origins in the
Gaelic word 'Cnoc' which means a hill. Village names which
end in 'shader' indicate a grazing area or pasture. This
comes from the Norse word 'saeter'.

All of the village names on this map are given in their
English spelling. However, as you travel through Point
you will see bilingual road signs which also give the Gaelic
version e.g. Pabail Uarach – Upper Bayble.

The variety of placenames in Point is a reflection of the
diverse and interesting history which makes the area so
special.

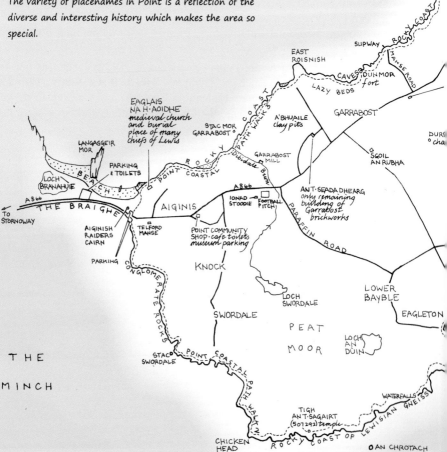

BROAD
BAY

GEO
EATH
and
for
boa

GOB
HUNISGEIR

SLIPWAY

ROCKY COAST

TANSE ROAD

EAST
ROISNISH

CAVES · DUNMOR
fort

LAZY BEDS

GARRABOST

DURS
o cha

EAGLAIS
NA H·AOIDHE
medieval church
and burial
place of many
chiefs of Lewis

STAC MOR
GARRABOST

A'BHUAILE
clay pits

LANGASGEIR
MOR

ROCKY

PATH WALKS

POINT COASTAL

Dibidale Burn

GARRABOST
MILL

SGOIL
AN RUBHA

PARKING
& TOILETS

BEACH

LOCH
BRANAHUIE

A866

THE BRAIGHE

AIGINIS

A866

IONAD
STOODIE

FOOTBALL
PITCH

AN T·SEADA DHEARG
only remaining
building of
Garrabost
brickworks

PARAFFIN ROAD

To
STORNOWAY

AIGINISH
RAIDERS
CAIRN

TELFORD
MANSE

POINT COMMUNITY
SHOP · cafe toilets
museum parking

PARKING

KNOCK

CONGLOMERATE ROCKS

LOWER
BAYBLE

EAGLETON

LOCH
SWORDALE

SWORDALE

PEAT

MOOR

LOCH
AN
DUIN

THE

MINCH

STAC
SWORDALE

POINT COASTAL PATH WALK 2

WATERFALLS

ROCKY COAST OF LEWISIAN GNEISS

TIGH
AN T·SAGAIRT
(507292) temple

CHICKEN
HEAD

ROCKY COAST OF LEWISIAN GNEISS

o AN CHROTACH

TIUMPAN HEAD LIGHTHOUSE

Tom Clark

The lighthouse at Tiumpan Head began operating on 1 December 1900. It was designed by David and Charles Stevenson and the main contractor was John Aitken. The cost of constructing the 21-metre tower, with optics by Chance Brothers, was £9000. The light, which flashes twice every 15 seconds, was operated by mains electricity with a battery back-up in case of power cuts. The clockwork apparatus for turning the lens had to be wound by hand every 35 minutes.

The lighthouse was visited by the Queen, Prince Charles and Princess Anne in 1956, on which occasion the 7-year old prince sounded the new foghorn for the first time. This was operated by an air compressor driven by a Kelvin diesel engine.

There were originally six keepers attached to the lighthouse, three of whom lived in the attached cottages with their families. An assistant and three occasional keepers lived locally. The lighthouse was automated in 1985, and the cottages are now used as a cat and dog home.

Tiumpan Head is an excellent vantage point from which to spot passing whales, dolphins and porpoises, but care must be taken when walking round the clifftops, especially in wet weather. On top of the hill beside the lighthouse is a walled wartime construction with a sheltered picnic table.

Historical information from Northern Lighthouse Board website www.nlb.org.uk.

Aerial view of Tiumpan Head Lighthouse   *Chris Murray*

Bayble Beach and Pier   *Janet Cameron*

PIERS AROUND POINT
Alex John Murray

Bayble Pier Bayble was looked upon as an important fishing centre in the Eye Peninsula, and in 1883 crofter/fishermen from Bayble and Garrabost gave evidence to a government backed committee about the need for a pier at Bayble. They told how more than 12 years previously Sir James Matheson's men had came and destroyed the original stone pier; the stones were removed and taken by steamer to Stornoway for use on his estate. They explained that the proposed new pier at Bayble would be of benefit to the neighbouring villages of Garrabost, Sheshader and Knock and would make Bayble a fishing station in the summer months. However it took until the 1st of April 1898 before the Congested District Board made a grant offer of £1,640 for the present concrete pier, which was paid out on completion in March 1903. From Bayble Pier the following grounds were fished: Chicken Rock, Old Adam (Eilean na Crothach), Bible Head (Bayble Head), Black Sandy (Dun Dubh) and Tiumpan Head for herring, mackerel, cod, ling, conger eel, skate, haddock, coley, pollack, plaice, lobster and crab. Most of the catches were processed in the curing stations/salting houses on site, before being sold to the markets.

In 1901 the board also made £270 available for a landing place at **Shader** (Shulishader) which consists of a concrete apron with steps leading down the cliff face.

Sheshader Shore   *Christeen Mackenzie*

Portnaguran   *Liz Chaplin*

A small narrow slipway was constructed at **Sheshader** in 1970, with further widening and a winch for hauling boats up to the top of the slip added in 2001 at a cost of £30,000.

The Walpole Commission recommended a beacon be placed on the Hen and Chicken Rock at a cost of £355; the work was carried out under the Western Highlands and Islands Works Act.

Portnaguran Pier Although the sum of £1,625 was granted for the building of this pier prior to March 31st 1898, to be paid out of the Western Highlands and Islands Works Act, a local contribution of £138. 19s. 7d. was also required. The offer was not taken up by the crofter/fishermen in the village at that time and the present pier was constructed about 1952. However it is only suitable for small open boats, which can be hauled up on the beach at the first sign of bad weather. The grounds fished are Tiumpan Head, the whole of Broadbay and Tolsta Head, again catching the same species as at Bayble.

It was also resolved that the committee should support the application of the Ross-shire County Council for a grant to construct a pier at **Swordale** in close proximity to the proposed village at Aignish. (This may well be the small concrete landing place at Cladach Suardal).

The latest addition in 2005 to Bayble, is the mooring basin **Papastaidh**, which is to the NE of the concrete pier and to the East of the former fish curing/salting station, which has been rebuilt and converted to a store and toilet. The main purpose of creating this basin was to provide a safe haven in all weathers for small leisure boats, as well as commercial fishing boats of up to 25ft. Grant funding was provided by various government and Western Isles Council bodies totalling £225,000.

The steam trawler "Ferrol" which ran aground near Sheshader, photograph with permission from Eilean an Fraoich

THE WRECKS OF POINT
Alasdair Macleod

To some, the phrase above might conjure up visions of crusty, inebriated Rubhachs staggering around the celebrated watering-holes of Stornoway. Although there are some colourful, living "wrecks" to be found on the Eye Peninsula, this article is concerned with the many fascinating maritime wrecks to be found on the shores and seabed around Point.

A glance at the map of Point today provides much evidence that the Peninsula has been visited by seafarers from distant lands for many centuries. The remains of a chambered cairn and standing stone circle in Garrabost moor at Cnoc na Dursainen are thought to date back over 2,000 years. We know that the Vikings visited Point from placenames such as Shader (Saetr meaning pasture) and Garrabost (bost meaning farm). Also the remains of three ancient "duns" or forts can be found in lochs at Aird and Eagleton and at the Dun Dubh headland at Sheshader. The ancient ruined temple near Chicken Head and other historical sites such as Ui Church on the Braighe all indicate that the Eye Peninsula has been a regular port of call for many seafarers down the ages.

Due to the almost constant battering our area receives in the winter months from extreme weather, it is quite unlikely that many ancient wrecks have been left intact on the sea floor. However, by chance, in 1989 the discovery of the remains of eleven bodies buried in a sand dune on the Braighe provided some direct evidence of the strong possibility of a foreign shipwreck.

The remains or skeletons were uncovered in the course of road improvements to the main Point-Stornoway road at the Point end of the Braighe. Edinburgh University Archaeology Department identified the remains as being those of males between their late teens and early thirties. Seventeen coins were found at the burial site and these included Scottish coins from the reign of Charles II (1660-1685). The foreign coins were from Ireland, Holland and Austria. The diversity of coins suggests that it is very likely that the deceased were foreigners. It is possible that they were the crew of a Dutch boat as the Dutch fished extensively for herring in Lewis waters in the 17th and early 18th centuries. Two main types of vessels were used at this time. The smaller "twelve tunnes" which were manned by 5/6 people and the larger vessels, called "busses", which were 75' long and carried an optimum crew of fifteen.

The other factor which suggests that the crew were foreigners is that they were buried outwith St Columba's graveyard which is literally a stone's throw from where the remains were found. We shall probably never know the name of the shipwreck, but it is possible that one day some local divers might come across the remains of the vessel from which the unfortunate eleven mariners had come.

Moving on to the 19th century, the story of the schooner or schooner brig "Jane" which landed at Swordale in 1821 is one of the most fascinating of all Hebridean sea yarns. This is a true story of mutiny and murder on the high seas and another example of how the truth is very often stranger than fiction. Although the story ended in Swordale, Point it began on 19th May 1821 when the "Jane" left Gibraltar bound for Bahia in Brazil with a cargo of 20 pipes of sweet oil, 34 bales of paper, 98 barrels of beeswax, 15 bags of aniseed, 300 jars of olives, boxes of raisins, and last, but not least, 38,180 Spanish silver dollars.

Some days out of Gibraltar a plot was hatched between Francis Gautiez, the French cook and Peter Heaman, the mate, who was an Englishman, to seize control of the ship and silver by murdering the Captain. On the evening of 7th June 1821 the conspirators shot the Captain and clubbed Paterson, the most senior and responsible seaman on the ship, to death. Attempts were then made to kill two other Scottish crew members, called Smith and Strachen, but they were allowed to live after being forced to swear on the Bible that they would never expose the murderers. Another seaman, Dhura, an Italian, and Camelier, the Maltese cabin boy, were sufficiently frightened that they were not considered a threat by the mutineers. The bodies of the murdered seamen were dumped overboard and the mate then set sail for the west coast of Scotland.

Eventually, around the 1st July, the "Jane" arrived at Barra and the mate, calling himself Captain Rogers, went ashore for supplies. Apart from the provisions of a sheep, six geese, five ducks and some butter, the mate also bought an open boat with sail.

The "Jane" then headed North with the intention of sailing round to the east coast of Scotland. While in Barra the mate heard of the presence of a revenue cutter in the Minch and it is possible that this is what influenced the mutineers' next decision. When off Chicken Head, near Swordale, the small boat purchased in Barra was loaded up with the dollars, packed in canvas bags, and some provisions. Holes were made in the side of the "Jane" in preparation for scuttling her. The mutineers' intention, it would appear, was to make for the mainland in the small boat, but at this stage things started to go wrong.

The "Jane", instead of sinking, drifted away and was eventually driven ashore at Tolsta Head. The mutineers, instead of crossing the Minch, had to make for a sheltered beach under the Swordale rocks due to unfavourable sea conditions.

The crew set up camp on a small shingle beach not far from Chicken Head. However they were not left undisturbed for long as word was soon sent to the Custom House officials in Stornoway. When Mr Maciver, the Custom's Officer, arrived at the mutineers' camp, he was met by the mate who must have concocted a very plausible story for Mr Maciver, on hearing the mate's tale, set off back for Stornoway.

The story goes that he had only proceeded a short distance up the cliff path when the Maltese cabin boy chased after him and blurted out the true story. The Custom's Officer believed the boy's story for the Officer later returned with reinforcements and arrested the mutineers. They were taken under guard to the court in Stornoway and charged with their crimes. The mutineers' possessions and the silver dollars were transported to Stornoway the following day by horse and cart.

When the dollars were counted, almost 7,000 were missing from the original total. What became of the missing dollars? For many years afterwards Spanish silver dollars used to appear in Stornoway on market days!

And what happened to the mutineers? On the 9th January 1822, Gautiez and Heaman were hanged on the sands of Leith following the trial in which the rest had turned King's evidence.

One of the wrecks most often visited by divers in this area is the wreck of the HMS "Lively" which sank after hitting Chicken Rock on the 7th June 1883. The remains of the vessel are still evident, scattered over the seabed at the base of Chicken Rock. The "Lively" was a 1,000 ton wooden steam yacht built in 1870 with 250 hp engines and paddle wheels, as well as sails. She had a crew of more than 70 and had been used initially to carry supplies to relieve people who were suffering from famine in parts of Ireland.

The importance of the "Lively" lay in the fact that this was the ship which carried the Napier Commissioners round the crofting counties gathering evidence on the conditions of crofters at this time. A Royal Commission on Crofting had been established in 1883 under the chairmanship of Lord Napier. The Commissioners held meetings in 61 different places and interviewed 775 different people, most of whom gave their evidence in Gaelic. The culmination of the Commissioners' work was the passing of the Crofters' Act in 1886.

The events leading up to the sinking of the "Lively" are as follows. On the 7th June 1883, the Commissioners held a meeting in Lionel and then boarded the "Lively" for the voyage to Stornoway where the next meeting was to be held.

According to tradition, the "Lively" struck the then unmarked Chicken Rock although the weather and sea-state were good. She stuck fast on the jagged pinnacle of Chicken Rock, but there was no panic and the Commissioners and crew were able to take to the lifeboats. A passing steamer, called the "Mary Ann", rescued those in lifeboats and took them to Stornoway. When the tide went out the stern of the "Lively" sank and left her bow out of the water on the rock. The bow section was later towed into Stornoway Harbour.

People from the neighbouring village of Swordale gathered rich pickings from the "Lively" as tables, doors, masts and bits of the deck were washed ashore on the nearby beaches.

Moving on to more modern times, several ships have been wrecked around the Point coastline this century. The area around Tiumpan Head in particular has been the scene of many maritime disasters.

In May 1920, the 89 ton motor ketch "Greenland", bound for Belfast from Norway with a cargo of Archangel tar, was wrecked two miles NW of the lighthouse. The steam drifter "Convallaria" from Banff finally foundered west of the lighthouse in heavy weather in February 1924, after initially hitting a submerged rock on the Tolsta side of Broad Bay.

On 18th December 1931, the steam trawler "Ferrol" from Fleetwood ran aground at Dun Dubh, near Sheshader. The trawler became wedged in a crevice in the cliffs and after attempts were made to draw attention to their plight with flares and a bonfire, the only option left was to scale the cliffs. The mate volunteered to climb the steep rocks in the pitch dark and driving rain. Eventually, with the help of villagers from Sheshader, the eleven crew were saved.

The coal steamer "Golfer" also ended up on rocks at Sheshader in September 1932, but the ten crew members were all saved. The drifter called the "Glide" from Stornoway ended up at the bottom of the sea in the vicinity of the lighthouse in July 1934 also, but her demise was caused by fire. Luckily the nine crew were saved by other drifters in the sea at the time.

HMS "Lively" which sank near Chicken Head, image from the National Library of Scotland

The remains of another trawler the "Wyre Law" from Fleetwood can still be seen to this day about 3/4 of a mile west of Portnaguran Pier. The trawler was bound for the Minch fishing grounds on 23rd October 1952 when she ran aground in a south easterly Force 8 gale. The thirteen crew were saved but the vessel itself was a total loss.

This is by no means an exhaustive list of the Wrecks of Point, but rather an attempt to show the diversity of ships which have floundered in this locality during the last few centuries. Famous historical wrecks, such as the "Lively", although dispersed over a wide area, still act as a magnet for divers, not only because of the interesting artefacts still to be found around the base of the Chicken Rock, but also because of the richness and abundance of sea life in this area of the sea floor.

Many other wrecks are now just small lumps of battered, barnacled metal covered in layers of kelp, unrecognisable from previous times, when they sailed as proud vessels on the waters of the Minch. These twisted remains littering the sea bed now provide cosy, camouflaged homes for the steely eyed congers which divers often encounter in these localities. Few areas of the Lewis and Harris coastline are without their own wrecks and behind the demise of each wreck there is an interesting story to be told. These stories have kept generations of islanders entertained in years gone by and they still retain their fascination, even to this day.

Stornoway Gazette, Friday 25th December 1931

FLEETWOOD TRAWLER WRECKED AT SHESHADER

About 8.25am on Friday last, the Stornoway lifeboat was called out to the assistance of a trawler which had run aground near the village of Sheshader. The lifeboat left immediately, and the rocket apparatus was taken to Sheshader by the coastguard. When the lifeboat arrived at the scene they found the trawler's deck awash, only the wheelhouse, mast and funnel being above the water. Seeing people moving about on the shore, the lifeboat hailed them through the megaphone. They learned that the crew of the trawler had been able to make their way ashore without help.

The trawler was the Fleetwood registered Ferrol FD124, skippered by Robert Stafford. About 6am she was ashore at Sheshader. It was so dark at that time that the crew could not very well see what their situation was, so they fired several rockets and then made a bonfire of one of the trawls on the forecastle head, and lit flares on the stern. By the light of the bonfire they were able to see that the Ferrol was lying in a crevice between high cliffs.

Soon it became apparent that they would have to abandon her, and the Captain asked for volunteers to take a look ashore. The mate offered himself for the perilous task of scaling the steep cliffs in pitch darkness and driving rain. He was able to jump from the forepeak to the rocks, and climbing up some way, he made his rope fast to a boulder or jag of rock. With the rope to guide them and steady them if they lost a foothold, the rest of the crew followed the mate up to the ledge. The skipper was the last to leave, and a few moments after he got a foothold ashore, the Ferrol was swept from end to end by a heavy sea.

The skipper joined the crew on the ledge and took a second rope further up the cliff. The climb was stiff and dangerous, and some of the men had to wait on a ledge until daybreak.

One man reaching the top before the others, and striking across the moor in search of assistance at last reached Bayble, three miles away. The moor is wet and very broken, and he was quite worn out when he reached the village. Meanwhile, some people from Sheshader, which was only a mile distant from the place where the Ferrol struck, were attracted by the flare and went to see what was wrong. They reached the place shortly after the rest of the crew had succeeded in climbing the cliff, and they conducted them to the village.

In Sheshader the crew of the Ferrol were fed and clothed, for early breakfast had been prepared aboard when she struck, and they had to leave without food and in such clothes as they happened to be wearing at the time. The skipper and his men were loud in their praise of the hospitality shown them in Sheshader. "We will never forget their kindness" they said. In the afternoon the crew were conveyed to Stornoway, and housed at the Seaman's Mission. Necessary articles of clothing were supplied them by ex-provost Murdo Maclean, the local agent for the Shipwrecked Mariners' Society and all but the skipper left Stornoway on Friday night for Fleetwood. Despite their adventure none of the men suffered anything more serious than scratches.

An earlier version of this article was in the Eilean An Fraoich Annual, published by the Stornoway Gazette.

Wreck of the "Wyre Law", Flesherin   *Tom Clark*

Aignish Cairn *Liz Chaplin*

AIGNISH RIOT
Alasdair Macleod

After crossing the Braighe isthmus to Point, on the left hand side of the road on the approach to the village of Aignish, there is a prominent monument consisting of two striking stone pillars. For many first-time visitors to An Rubha, the Gaelic name for Point, their initial question is about this monument and what it signifies. This monument or cairn is a memorial to all those who were involved in the Aignish Riot of January 9 1888, which was part of the historic struggle by crofters throughout the Highlands and Islands for Land Law Reform.

The inscription on the plaque at the Aignish Cairn states "This cairn was erected in memory of the men and women of Point who raided the farm at Aignish on January 9, 1888. They did so because they were driven beyond endurance by destitution and oppression. Instead of acting to relieve their distress, the authorities used the majesty of the law and the armed might of the military to crush the people. "Thirteen of the raiders were sentenced to prison with terms ranging from 6 months to 15 months." Although the raid technically ended in failure, the plight of the starving crofters was drawn to a wider national audience and, in 1905, Aignish farm was officially broken into 32 crofts. At the end of the day, the crofters' struggle was not in vain, although it was later generations who reaped the reward of the historic events of 1888.

The Aignish Riot and other manifestations of land agitation had their roots in the decades of harsh and insensitive treatment meted out by landlords intent on maximising profits from deer forests and sheep farms. In an era when land agitation was common in Lewis, no incident was as violent or premeditated as the Aignish Riot. On January 9, 1888, the fields of Aignish farm became a battlefield as up to a thousand crofters and landless cottars, male and female, clashed with the Sheriff, police and detachments of Royal Scots and Marines. Trouble had been brewing in the Point district, for some time, with the focus of land agitation being on the fertile Aignish farm tenanted by Samuel Albany Newhall. On the 24th and 29th December 1887, two mass meetings had been held in Point, one at Garrabost Free Church, where the decision had been taken to seize Aignish farm. Another grievance which the crofters had was that the Aignish farm tenant had been using the Ui Cemetery as a fank for his sheep and cattle.

However, the political establishment soon got wind of the plans to take over the farm and, in the first week of January 1888, Stornoway's Sheriff-substitute posted up Gaelic and English notices which warned participants that the proposed occupation of the farm would be illegal and leave those involved open to heavy penalties. It became evident that the crofters were intent on taking over Aignish farm, and steps were taken by the forces of law and order to prepare for the worst possible scenario.

Sheriff Fraser and Procurator Fiscal John Ross from Stornoway requested a substantial force to ensure that the potential revolt would be dealt with effectively. On Sunday 8 January 1888, 18 police constables were deployed to Aignish farmhouse and outbuildings but were instructed to remain under cover. Eighty Marines and Royal Scots were put at Sheriff Fraser's disposal. In the small hours of Monday morning, HMS Seahorse landed the marines in Sandwick Bay under the command of Captain Plumb.

At 11am, the crofters appeared as planned, and soon, several hundred men and women marched from the village to the farmhouse, armed with sticks and assorted bludgeons – but no weapons. The raiders scattered all over the farmlands. At this stage, the Sheriff and Procurator Fiscal decided to intervene and the Riot Act was read to the raiders in Gaelic and they were asked to disperse peaceably. When it became obvious that the raiders did not intend to disperse, the police were called into action and the Marines appeared from the farm buildings with bayonets drawn. Inevitably, fighting broke out and arrests were made indiscriminately. Even then, peace was not restored as desperate efforts were made by the raiders to free the arrested men.

A squad of Royal Scots were summoned from their position at Melbost to ensure that those arrested could be taken to jail in Stornoway. The procession of policemen, soldiers, Marines and prisoners eventually set off for the town under the fusillade of sticks, stones and clods of earth from the jeering crowd of crofters incensed that the violent confrontation had not resulted in achieving their aim of taking over Aignish farm. This would be eventually achieved, but not until 1908.

Looking beyond the Cairn and back into history, it is obvious that the people of Point were decent, law-abiding citizens, pushed beyond the limits of their tolerance by the poverty of their squalid economic and social conditions. These so-called rioters were not challenging the might of the political establishment in pursuit of ideological principles – they were there, face to face with the Sheriff and the Riot Act, because they were literally starving. Their only goal was a share of the survival currency of the day, which was land. They were not after vast chunks of land but small parcels of Aignish farmland which would provide them with the basic means of survival. The Aignish Cairn is a type of bridge with the past which allows us a glimpse of the historical forces which shaped our current landscape.

Peat bank　　　　　　　　　　　　　　　　　　*John Murray, Stornoway*

THE LEWIS CHEMICAL WORKS
Dr Ali Whiteford

In 1842 James Matheson returned from the Far East where, along with his business partner William Jardine, he had amassed a vast fortune. Two years later when Matheson purchased the Isle of Lewis he had two objectives in mind: one was the improvement of the living conditions of the inhabitants after the disastrous potato famine and the second was to develop and exploit the abundant natural resources of the island. Matheson was keen on science and was enthusiastic about new ideas. So when an employee named Henry Caunter, who was a keen amateur scientist, started carrying out experiments on the distillation of peat which showed commercial promise, Matheson financed the venture. The Lewis Chemical Works was created in 1857 and ran as a commercial enterprise until 1875.

In the process peat was cut, dried and then distilled. To distil peat it is heated but without air so that it does not burn; instead it undergoes a chemical reaction and changes to produce various substances, the main ones being a thick tar, a watery liquid, an inflammable gas and a solid coke-like residue. At the time, distillation was an important process for the production of useful substances. Many substances were distilled, principally coal which produced creosote for treating wood used in the expanding railway industry; paraffin as a replacement for animal oil for lamps; and wax for candles.

Henry Caunter's first experiments were carried out next to an ornamental fish pond near Lews Castle. Tar was produced but fish were killed and the works were moved outside the castle grounds near to the Creed Lodge. A canal was built to transport peat to the works and about half a ton of tar was produced in two years. Caunter had little practical skill and so, in 1859, Dr. Benjamin Horatio Paul was appointed as chemist in charge of the chemical works, to design and construct an operational works on a commercial scale with the principal aim of producing paraffin. He redesigned Caunter's works and moved them 100 yards south to afford easier access to the peat banks which were connected to the works by 3 miles of tramway.

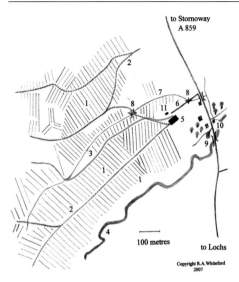

The main site of the Lewis Chemical Works

1 Peat banks. The peat was cut, dried and stacked in the same way as for domestic peat. Cutting took place from May to September although the Works was in operation continuously.

2 Tramway. Over three miles of tramway were laid through the moor. Originally, the small wagons were man-handled but later on a steam winch was used. There is evidence that ponies were used at Garrabost.

3 Canal. This was used to transport peat to Caunter's original works. Parts of this still exist.

4 River Creed.

5 Lewis Chemical Works.

6 Cartway. The peat tar was allowed to cool in tar pits and then taken by horse and cart to Garrabost.

7 Stream.

8 Bridge site.

9 Car park with memorial plaque incorporating tramway line and Garrabost brick.

10 Creed Lodge. Donald Morison, builder, operational foreman and chronicler of the Lewis Chemical Works lived here.

11 Caunter's original works.

Initial trials were a failure as a result of poor kiln and condenser design and alterations were made. Paul had been involved in the development of the Irish Peat Co. in the 1840s, one of the first commercial schemes designed to produce paraffin from peat. His design for the Lewis works bore great similarity to that of the Irish works yet, curiously, he omitted all-important safety valves which led to a large explosion which, luckily, produced no fatalities. Paul sought help and redesigned the condensers and draughting and by the autumn of 1861 the results were encouraging.

The works were not very environmentally friendly! Major problems occurred with pollution of the river Creed by the watery liquid produced in the process which killed salmon fry in this important fishing river. The prevailing winds blew the obnoxious gases produced by the process over the nearby town of Stornoway and the operating of the process was extremely hazardous to the health of the workmen who were regularly overcome by fumes when charging the kilns. In time the watery liquid was disposed of in a controlled way although a large proportion was used to produce fertiliser for the development of the grounds of Lews castle. The problem of the smelly exhaust gas was solved when an accident led to the discovery that the gas burned. It was then used as a source of heat to raise steam and to help keep the kilns hot.

There were ready markets for the crude tar: in Glasgow as a heavy lubricant for axles and in Liverpool as an anti-fouling agent for ships' hulls. Henry Caunter took out patents for these uses in 1863 and 1864. In the 1850s, James Young had started producing paraffin oil for lighting from shale mined in the Lothians. By 1861, when Young's patent on the process had run out, other operators moved in and the distillation of shale was carried out on a vast scale. It was discovered that the addition of refined peat tar would greatly improve the burning of this shale oil and the operators would take all the peat tar they could get.

However, Paul's aim all along had been to produce paraffin from peat. This involved taking the peat tar and refining it in much the same way as, nowadays, crude oil from the North Sea is refined to make the products with which we are familiar - petrol, diesel paraffin, etc. Paul developed a refinery on the site of Caunter's original works and as a result produced a saleable lighting paraffin oil which was sold in Glasgow under the brand name '*Lignole*' at a competitive price. Refining also produced pitch which was suitable for roofing and as a coal substitute and finally candle wax. It is said that the first paraffin wax candles burned in the Houses of Commons were produced from Hebridean peat tar and burned with a bright, odourless flame. When in operation, the Lewis Chemical Works were known locally as the Candle Works. While Paul was developing the Chemical Works and the refinery he was developing a larger refinery at Garrabost, some 8 miles from the Lewis Chemical Works. This was the site of the Brick Works established by Matheson in 1844 to make bricks and tiles from the abundant natural deposits of clay in the area. The extensive covered sheds provided a suitable site for the expensive refinery although an extension had to be built in the glen behind the Garrabost Mill to site stills as there was not enough water at the brickworks. Water was essential for the operation of the stills and as a raw material.

Demand for the products was high; the markets for the peat tar seemed broad and endless as were the tracts of peatland providing the raw material for the process itself. All seemed to be set for James Matheson to make another fortune and realise his hopes for the island and its inhabitants.

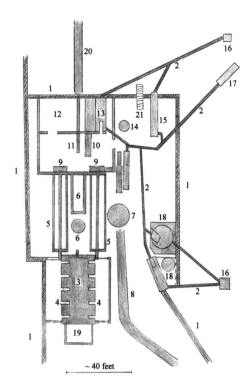

Ground plan of the Lewis Chemical Works showing the brick foundations, gas flues and tramways

1 retaining wall
2 gas flues
3 kilns
4 ash pits
5 seats for condensers
6 receiving and settling tanks
7 vat
8 tramway to tar pits
9 condensers
10 steam engine
11 drum for rope hauling machine
12 store
13 steam boiler
14 grease mill
15 lime furnace
16 stack
17 gas burner
18 evaporating boilers
19 lime store
20 tramway to peat banks (continues over the kilns)
21 stair

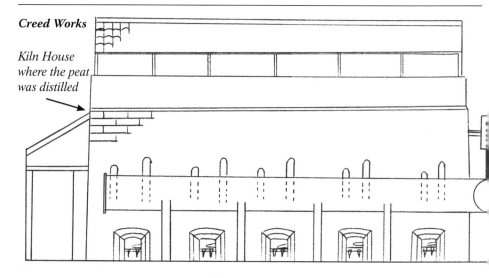

Creed Works

Kiln House where the peat was distilled

In 1862 Paul suddenly left the works. Whether he was frustrated at the lack of progress and the vagaries of the weather or the workforce or his own thwarted ambitions is not known. Perhaps he was fleeing from a ladyfriend; the oral tradition of Garrabost suggests this may be the case. The most likely reason is the discovery of crude oil in the U.S.A. and the subsequent import of paraffin which, within three years, was to bring crisis to the paraffin industry. Paul, who was a rising star in the communication of matters scientific, including energy technology, probably saw the writing on the wall and left to pursue a brilliant career in the world of pharmaceutics.

Paul's departure signalled a change in the development and running of the Lewis Chemical Works: business management practice, commercial venturism and scientific research were to take on new meanings. James MacFadyen was a brick-maker at Garrabost who was working his notice due to constant insobriety, fired by Paul just before Paul left. By dint of flattery, blarney and guile, MacFadyen was appointed chemist, with Henry Caunter elevated to the position of general manager. Caunter, although an enthusiastic and ambitious amateur, had little business enterprise or leadership qualities and was easily deceived and manipulated by the wily MacFadyen. It took a while for the pair to figure out how to make saleable lighting oil, in the process causing bad pollution of the fishing and shoreline of Broad Bay. MacFadyen soon realised that there was a ready market for the product on his doorstep - the local villages around Broad Bay - which could be supplied on a cash-only, no-records basis. The problem for MacFadyen was that the crude tar was being sold directly from the Creed Works to the markets on the mainland - as an anti-fouling agent, as axle grease and for the shale oil industry: only part of the tar was refined at Garrabost. MacFadyen proceeded to sabotage the markets and divert all the crude tar to Garrabost. The grease market was scuppered by adulterating the tar with water. Next, MacFadyen convinced the impressionable Caunter that refining the tar improved its anti-fouling properties and backed up his assertion with bogus results from contrived experiments. The resulting pitch that was sent to Liverpool was unfit as an anti-fouling agent and orders were stopped enabling MacFadyen to produce more paraffin for his local

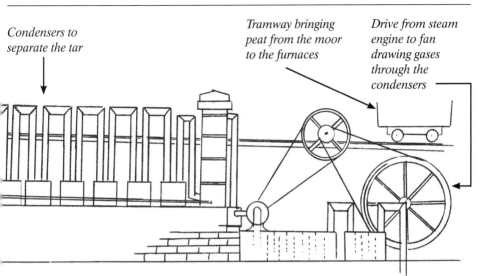

Condensers to separate the tar

Tramway bringing peat from the moor to the furnaces

Drive from steam engine to fan drawing gases through the condensers

markets. It suited Caunter not to send the tar to the Shale works - he was spending large sums of James Matheson's money on an improved refinery for the unrealistic objective of extracting dyes from peat. This would be redundant if all the tar was sold. MacFadyen encouraged Caunter in this project as it kept Caunter away from the Garrabost refinery: he even interfered with Caunter's experimenting to give the impression that results were positive. MacFadyen was eventually found out and in 1869 he left and with his large family emigrated to America, leaving his brother in charge at Garrabost. The Lewis Chemical Works carried on until 1874 when it was shut down.

How did this apparently chaotic enterprise manage to survive for so long? James Matheson, who was in his declining years, was a hands-off proprietor, preferring to leave the running of his businesses to his managers which allowed Caunter to pursue his own interests rather than discharge his responsibilities. The refinery at Garrabost, where MacFadyen was in charge, gave employment to a number of people at a time when paid work was scarce. Perhaps he was some sort of Robin Hood character dispersing part of the proceeds from his clandestine commercial venture to the needy locals who would be only too keen to keep him in post - one worker was actually dismissed for trying to expose the dishonesty.

The Lewis Chemical Works was important. Although its commercial success cannot be gauged, it provided many islanders with desperately needed employment for nearly twenty years. We are lucky that this intriguing tale of Victorian enterprise survives, chronicled in 1897 by the works foreman, Donald Morison of Stornoway, who was also the builder of the Works and who successfully developed and kept them running after Paul left. His journal tells a story full of incident, drama, comedy, farce and pathos, inhabited by what appear to be variously scoundrels, buffoons, gentry, academics and Hebridean heroes. Dr Paul presented papers on the development of the Lewis Chemical Works to the British Association and to the Society of Arts although, in later life, he appears to have chosen to forget his time in Lewis.

What remains of the Lewis Chemical Works? A large part of the Garrabost brickworks remains standing; a substantial building built, naturally, of Garrabost brick. The miles of

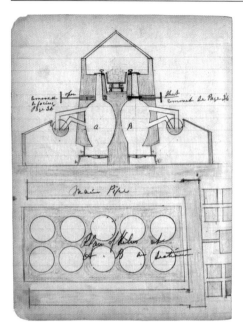

A sketch of the kilns designed by Paul, taken from Donald Morison's journal.

Dr Benjamin Horatio Paul, a man of many talents and achievements, who became editor of the Pharmaceutical Journal for many years.

The Museum of the Royal Pharmaceutical Society

tramway line were recycled as fence posts and can be seen around the Marybank area of Stornoway. There are echoes in various geographical locations. Peat banks near the site of the works which are cut for domestic fuel are still referred to as the paraffin banks. The corner of the main road at the Cabarfeidh Hotel and opposite the house where Henry Caunter lived is known as Caunter's Corner. At Garrabost, there are places called Garadh Pol (Paul's enclosure) and Buaile Macphadhain (MacFadyen's enclosure) as well as the Paraffin Road leading to Bayble.

Main site of Lewis Chemical Works   Eilidh Whiteford

1 *The site of Caunter's original works. Caunter produced tar only with the assistance of a local named Wilson who had a reputation for ingenuity. Wilson had been involved with the Gas Works in Stornoway and so would have had knowledge of distillation. Caunter came from Ashburton, near Exmoor in Devon, where attempts to distil peat had been successful.*

2 *The Site of Paul's works. It was built on the top of the hill despite requiring water.*

3 *Line of Tramway to the tar pits.*

4 *Cartway from the main road to Caunter's works which became the first refinery.*

5 *Stream which flows to the River Creed. This stream took much pollution from the works, killing salmon.*

6 *Tar pits where the tar was allowed to cool.*

The story of the Lewis Chemical Works remains an important episode in the history of Lewis: more a tale of toil and strife, of success and failure, of monies lost and made, of the adventure of enterprise but, above all, of man's quest for something new to improve himself and society that seems to drive the exploitation of natural resources.

It was the separation of the Lewis Chemical Works into three sites – one at the River Creed and two at the Garrabost Brick Works – that allowed James MacFadyen to run his own enterprise.

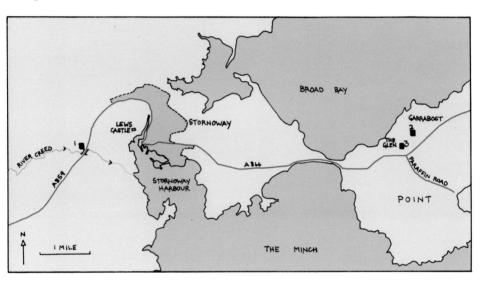

Map by Helen Macdonald

1 Lewis Chemical Works

2 Garrabost Brick Works

3 Stills

Donald Morison's account of the Lewis Chemical Works was written in 1895 just a couple of years before he died and over twenty years after the works ceased. He writes with passion and a dry humour and this is never more evident than when he describes the separation of the workings into three sites where his frustration at the situation is apparent: "in one word, an enormous, reckless blunder"

The author gratefully acknowledges the assistance he received from the late Frank Thompson, David Crabbe and Graham Morrison.

An t-Seada Dhearg,   *with permission from Cnoc Dubh Residents' Association*

BRICK MAKING AT CLAYPARK
Maggie Smith

This chapter is taken from a newsletter produced by Cnoc Dubh Residents' Association (Upper Garrabost) in 2006 to raise funds for a play area.

The Claypark Brick Works was one of a series of projects set up by Sir James Matheson who owned the Island of Lewis from 1844 till his death in 1878. The soil in Garrabost is derived from the Stornoway Formation - a mixture of conglomerates and sandstones which overlie the Lewisian Gneiss, especially between Aignish and Garrabost. The till contains clay and it is this which was used to make bricks and tiles. Claypark is part of Garrabost and the clay was dug in Upper Garrabost.

The Brick Works commenced on 1st March 1847 and they were managed by Dr Benjamin Horatio Paul; he also managed the nearby Chemical Works and the smithy at the Brick Works served the Chemical Works as well. Dr Paul set up his refining apparatus in a large shed at the Brick Works. In addition there was a smithy, cooperage, joinery shop and stables, all well fitted. The chief brickmaker came from Ireland and many of the people who worked in the Brick Works were from mainland Scotland. The census returns of 1851 and 1861 indicate workers and their families came from Ayrshire, Stirlingshire and Inverness-shire as well those born locally.

An t-Seada Dhearg or the red building is what remains of the original brickworks, although the 1851 map indicates a much larger building. Today the road runs through this area known as Claypark.

Bricks, roof and drain tiles were made from the Garrabost clay pit and when they were fired they were a distinctive red colour. The bricks were used for buildings throughout Lewis in the 1850-70s, including some of the island school buildings erected after the Education Act of 1872. The drainage tiles were used in Sir James Matheson's land improvement projects.

At Laxdale School on the outskirts of Stornoway, when the school teacher's accommodation was being linked to the new school building, a wall of red Lews Brick was discovered and it is still on display as a feature on the stairwell of the new building.

The bricks were also used at Leurbost School in Lochs, which opened in 1879 and was later demolished in 2001. In 2006 Mrs M. A. Kennedy, 103 years of age and a former teacher at the school said "I built an extension to my home, at the time Leurbost School was being knocked down. I picked up one of the red Lews Bricks as a keepsake and it is now to be seen built into the outside wall of my new extension".

It is known that red brick was used to build the Imperial Hotel on South Beach Street in Stornoway. This building became the Louise Carnegie Hostel, which was demolished many years ago. The An Lanntair building is now on that site.

Ardvourlie Castle in Harris has internal walls made of Lews brick. Lews Castle in Stornoway was being built by Sir James Matheson from 1847-1850. Although the external walls are made of stone, Lews Brick appears to have been used on the inside to pack those walls in some places. A few of the now exposed interior partitions of the castle are also in red brick. The bricks appear to have been utilised where they could be hidden, to pack other materials and then covered by roughcast, plaster or decorative facings.

There is a red brick building in Claypark, which is referred to as *An Sabhal ann am Buaile Choinnich Uilleam*. In oral tradition mention is made of a house in the glen *(Taigh Uilleam)* - William Macleod, who had come from Back. William is said to have had two sons *Coinneach Uilleam* and *Aonghas Uilleam* (Kenneth and Angus). After *Coinneach Uilleam*, the house was occupied by Donald Maciver, a headmaster at the local school, originally from Uig, Isle of Lewis. Donald Maciver wrote the emigrants' song *An Ataireachd Ard* and was a scholar interested in the derivation of local place names.

According to written tradition the Garrabost Smithy served both the Brickworks and the Garrabost site of the Lewis Chemical Works operation. The original *ceardach* or smithy was situated next to the present day outhouse, at The Corner House, Garrabost. Dr. Benjamin Horatio Paul is thought to have resided in a house on the site of The Corner House. The smithy was known in oral tradition as Vulcan Cottage. Red Lews Brick can be seen in the roadside gable of the existing outhouse, but the interior walls are built of stone.

The 1851 and 1861 census returns include frequent mention of men employed as Tile Manufacturers, Brick and Tile Makers and Brickmakers in relation to the Claypark Brickworks.

Excerpt from the Diary of John Munro Mackenzie, Chamberlain of the Lews, dated Friday 30th May 1851: *"Proceeded to Garrabost and remained there all day paying workmen and taking inventory of tools, iron and other articles at the Tile Work, discharged several of the work people, and gave others notice that their services would not be required after next month. As the drainage works are now about being completed and no demand for bricks or tiles. I fear these works must be thrown idle on account of the great expense of cartage to and from the works and high price which must be paid for coals, with other causes tiles cannot be made here so cheap as further south and if they have to be exported there will be an additional charge for freight."*

In 2006 a group of children from Garrabost chose a spot at the bottom of one of the pits; they removed the turf and the top layer of clay, until they reached the useable clay seam. They stored some clay in sealed containers until it dried out and became pliable.

Bricks were made using moulds, which were left to dry for several weeks. They were then fired in the Borve Pottery kiln and the bricks are now incorporated into the wall in the children's play area at *Cnoc Dubh*, Upper Garrabost.

Lews Brick in Laxdale School, with permission from Cnoc Dubh Residents' Association

Old clay pit, Garrabost   *Liz Chaplin*

Garrabost Mill

Graham Morrison

THE GARRABOST MEAL MILL
John Morrison

History

Shortly after the meal mill at Willowglen in Stornoway (Latta's Mill) was burned down, Lady Matheson granted a Charter in 1893 for ground at Allt-nan-Gall in Garrabost upon which to build a Meal Mill. Allt-nan-Gall would supply water for driving the Mill Wheel (roth mor a'mhuilinn). A sluice-gate was fitted to Loch Drollabhat near Swordale, and two earth dams were constructed, one near the Mill and one about 100 yards further up the burn from the main road.

The Mill was built at Garrabost for the benefit of crofters in the Point area. A Mill continued to operate at Gress to service the villagers on the other side of Broad Bay for a short time after the opening of the Garrabost Mill.

All the crofts in the various villages of Point, and indeed all over the island were fully cultivated producing considerable quantities of oats, barley, potatoes, and turnips. By far the commonest cereal crop at the turn of the century and until the Second World War was barley or bere.

The Mill buildings are constructed of stone quarried at Shader, Point, and the kiln and stable buildings of bricks manufactured at Claypark, Garrabost. The Garrabost brickworks had ceased production, but a ready supply of bricks was still available.

Shortly after the commencement of the First World War my late father, Angus Graham Morrison, originally of Habost, Ness, came from Vancouver to take over the running of the Mill. At that time, in 1914, the Garrabost Mill was very busy, often working day and night producing barley meal and oatmeal. The kiln peat fire was kept burning from Monday morning until Saturday evening during the season when most crofters came with their grain – October to February. The writer can well remember some crofters kiln-drying and milling as many as 10 or 12 sacks of grain each winter during the 1920s. From 10cwts (10 x 50 kilograms) of barley grain one could expect as much as 6 bolls (7.5 x 50 kilograms) of barley meal. The amount of meal produced from the same weight of oats is considerably less.

The grain crop was threshed either by suathadh (rubbing the grain with the feet), or by using the suist (flail), or with the aid of a small hand-powered threshing mill. The grain was winnowed on a day when there was a good breeze of wind, which carried away the loose chaff, small straws and dust. Having cleaned, prepared and bagged the barley or oats, the sacks were then marked by sewing on to each sack a piece of coloured wool or cloth. It was then taken to the kiln at the Mill where it was dried using good dry peats. This process took 4-5 hours, the grain being turned over at intervals to prevent burning. In some villages there was a small kiln and the writer can remember one at Aird and another at Portvoller.

Kiln Drying

The barley or oats must be dried for 4-5 hours until all the moisture is removed and the grain so hard that it can be cracked under the teeth. The kiln is fired with good dry peats. The grain is then re-bagged and transferred to the upper floor of the Mill.

Shelling and Sifting the Grain

The grain is first emptied into the hopper (an drabhailt) of the Shelling Stones (a mhuilinn sgilidh) on the upper level. As the grain falls through the eye of the stones (suil a mhuilinn) it passes between the rotating upper stone and the stationary nether stone. These are separated just sufficiently to crack the husk. Thereafter, it falls to the lower level down a chute on to the shelling sifter or rattler (criathair), which separates the dust (dudan) from the kernels or groats. This dust used to be in great demand for feeding to cattle along with boiled potatoes, though small by itself in energy value.

Winnowing

The grain falls over the end of the sifter into a strong breeze of wind, produced by a large fast-rotating fan, which carries away the husks (sgealbach). Sgealbach or chaff was sometimes fed to animals but has little nutritional value. It was also commonly used for filling pillows and mattresses.

Milling

Having finished the shelling, sifting and winnowing processes, the grain is now transferred back upstairs by an elevator to the hopper of the milling stones. The upper millstone weighs about 1 tonne, and as the grain passes between the runner and nether millstones it is ground into very fine meal. The coarseness or fineness of the meal can be varied by fractionally raising or lowering the upper millstone. The coarseness or fineness of the meal is judged by the miller between thumb and palm.

Sifting the Meal

The small amount of husk left adhering to the grain after shelling falls along with the meal into the meal sifter. This sifter (criathair na mine) moves with a rapid circular motion and separates the sids (ca) from the meal. The meal passes through two sifters incorporated into one frame-box, the end result is meal that is pure, clean, and free from any sids which fall into a separate bag. The bag of sids was always taken home along with the meal as it was considered good animal feeding.

The Garrabost Mill was constructed at a time when water mill technology had reached its peak. The dusty sifting and winnowing is screened off from the miller's working area, with the winnower having an external outlet (an important health consideration). The grain requires no handling whatsoever from the moment it is emptied into the shelling hopper until the full bag of meal is lifted away from the chute below the meal sifter. Consequently, although two men were needed to start the large oil engine, one man is sufficient to keep the Mill running.

Motive Power

Because there was a scarcity of water at times, a Simplex Oil Engine was purchased in 1908 and fitted to the Mill. This engine, manufactured at Leysmill near Arbroath, is a single piston engine burning paraffin fired by the early technology of hot tube ignition, and runs at 200 revolutions per minute. The piston diameter is 11 inches (280 millimetres), and stroke about 22 inches. It has been maintained in full working order. It is believed to be the only engine of its make still in existence, and one of only a few of its type. It is almost certainly the only engine manufactured in 1908 still occasionally used for the purpose for which it was originally installed. The Mill dam, which was constructed of stone, gravel and clay failed around 1932. This marked the end of water-power at Garrabost.

Memories

The writer well remembers how satisfied and thankful crofters were as they went home from the mill with three, four or even six bolls of meal. (A boll is 10 stones, or about 63 kg.) This represented the produce of a season's work, and a year's bread. Quite often, one boll or more was exchanged at the mill for a similar quantity of wheat flour. During the years around the 1920s, the Garrabost Mill was kept very busy serving the local crofters. One record kept in the year 1917 by my late father, Angus Graham Morrison, shows that 1,700 bolls or 106 tonnes of meal was produced in that year from locally grown grain for the people of Point. These were times when people were, of necessity, content with considerably less than is the case today. They were, however, in the writer's judgement, happy; and a community spirit of interdependence was a strong factor in this respect.

After the Second World War, the Lewis economy entered a period of rapid change. Crofts in rural Lewis ceased to be cultivated as men found other forms of employment. The Mill at Garrabost, in common with many up and down the country, was no longer needed and ceased production in 1956. It was restored to full working order in 1988 and many people now find it of interest. Some still enjoy the barley meal it produces.

Photo by Antonia James, www.food52.com

RECIPES FOR BARLEY MEAL
by Christine Morrison

BARLEY BANNOCKS – ARAN EORNA - Oven Recipe

Ingredients
1 lb barley meal
1 handful of flour (plain or sr)
½ teaspoon of salt.
1 teaspoonful cream of tartar
1 teaspoonful baking soda
3 oz margarine
1 tablespoon syrup

Method
1. Dissolve margarine and syrup in a little warm water
2. Mix the dry ingredients
3. Add the margarine and syrup mixture
4. Bind together with milk
5. Roll out thinly
6. Cook in a very hot oven.

www.shipton-mill.com

BARLEY BREAD
by Bread Machine. Makes 1 large loaf

Ingredients
1 large egg
200ml (7fl oz) milk
1 tsp easy-blend dried yeast
375g (13oz) strong white bread flour
125g (4oz) barley meal
1 tsp salt
2 tsp honey
25g (1oz) butter

Method
1. Lightly beat the egg in a measuring jug. Add the milk, then make up to 350ml (12fl oz) with water
2. Put the ingredients into the bread maker bucket, following any instructions in the machine manual
3. Fit the bucket into the bread maker and set to the basic programme. Press start
4. Just before baking starts make shallow diagonal cuts across the bread then repeat on the other diagonal to make a diamond pattern. (ALTERNATIVELY place the dough in a bread-pan and bake in your oven)
5. After baking, remove the bread from the machine (or oven) and shake out on a wire rack to cool.

Point War Memorial, Garrabost   *Liz Chaplin*

WORLD WAR 1 – THE POINT CONTRIBUTION
Alasdair Macleod

Formal recognition of the contribution made by servicemen from the Point district to World War 1 is to be found in the publication entitled - "Loyal Lewis" Roll of Honour and also on the plaques at the Point War Memorial.

The Point War Memorial is situated in the village of Garrabost, beside the Garrabost Church of Scotland. The War Memorial and Garden of Remembrance was created in 2004 after a community campaign spearheaded by the Point War Memorial Committee. Four memorial plaques are on one side of the walled, paved garden. The plaques commemorate those who fell in the two World Wars. The stonework of the memorial garden walls is constructed from the reclaimed stones from derelict black houses in the Peninsula. Some of these houses were originally the homes of those lost in the Wars and whose names are recorded on the memorial plaques. The information in this brief article refers only to the Great War or World War 1 and the information was obtained from the "Loyal Lewis" Roll of Honour 1914-18.

The opening paragraph in the "Loyal Lewis" publication relating to the Point district states:

"The rumours of war in the closing days of July 1914 were suddenly changed to its grim actualities when, on the 4th August, Great Britain formally made her entry into the greatest war in the world's history. Nearly all the young men of the district belonged to the Royal Naval Reserve or the "Militia". Consequently, the news that we were about to engage in mortal combat with the greatest military nation in the world was received with staggering amazement, quickly followed by calm resolution and determination to serve their King and country with all their powers of brain and arm. From this district there was an immediate response to the Nation's cry – "To Arms" – not only by those who were duty bound to go, but also by those who had no military training. Many of those were actually under military age, but, being big and sturdy, they pretended to be older than they really were, and their services were accepted. There was no need for conscription here."

It must be noted that, although there are no female names on the remembrance plaques, women played a hugely important role in the First World War. Women were not allowed technically to serve on the Frontline, but risked body and mind in the munitions factories which provided ammunition and bombs for the Frontline troops. These factories only paid lip service to rudimentary Health and Safety regulations and explosions in these factories were not uncommon.

All those who participated in the theatre of war were heroes and heroines whether they received special military recognition or not but it is impossible to mention the individual gallantry of all those from Point who served on land and sea for the principles of freedom. Even when peace came with the signing of the Armistice on 11th November 1918, there was still more heartbreak and hardship to come with the horror and sickening tragedy of the "Iolaire" on New Year's morning 1919, which to this day casts a dark, sombre shadow over our island community.

The "Loyal Lewis" Roll of Honour divides the contribution of Point servicemen into the three school districts of our Peninsula and this division is reflected in the format of this article.

According to Angus MacDonald, the Headteacher of Aird Public School, who was responsible for the input for the Aird School District in the Roll of Honour, 402 servicemen took part in the Great War. The Aird School District which included the villages of Portvoller, Aird, Sheshader, Shader, Flesherin, Portnaguran and Broker suffered 74 casualities in the course of the conflict. In terms of villages in the Aird School District, the Roll of Honour details are as follows:

TOWNSHIP	ROLL OF HONOUR	DEAD
Aird	74	12
Portvoller	61	10
Broker	22	4
Flesherin	44	7
Portnaguran	52	12
Sheshader	80	20
Shader	69	9

These are just dry statistics which do not take account of many acts of heroism and bravery. Christine Macleod from Portvoller, for example, was the Matron of the Highland Casualty Clearing Station Hospital in France and was awarded the prestigious Royal Red Cross medal. Alex Mackenzie, originally from Shader, became the Lieutenant Commander of USS "Los Angeles".

Possibly the most remarkable war story of all concerned Gunner Alick John MacDonald, son of Torquil MacDonald from 4 Portvoller. He was on the SS "Palm Branch" when his ship encountered two enemy submarines off the Kola Inlet in the Arctic Ocean near Russia on the 4th May 1917. He is credited with sinking one submarine and disabling the other due to his gunnery skills. On arrival at Archangel, he was presented with a Russian decoration for his bravery. Sadly, Alick John was lost at sea on the 25th November, 1917.

The Bayble School District included Upper and Lower Garrabost, Upper and Lower Bayble, Park and Geiler and the war efforts of the servicemen from this district were recorded by Donald MacIver, the Headteacher of Bayble Public School. According to the Roll of Honour, the number on military service during the war was 383 and of those, 83 died in the service of their country. The statistics for each village are as follow:

TOWNSHIP	ROLL OF HONOUR	DEAD
Upper Bayble	99	29
Lower Bayble	108	16
Geiler	28	5
Park	22	6
Upper Garrabost	48	11
Lower Garrabost	78	16

The "Iolaire" tragedy accounted for 10 lives in the Bayble School district and brought the total number of drowning in the conflict up to 30. Three young lads from the

Point War Memorial   *Liz Chaplin*

district – Allan Graham, Garrabost, Donald (Colin) Macleod, Upper Bayble and Malcolm (Kenneth) MacIver from Lower Bayble – all fell on the same day in the ill-fated advance up the Tigris.

The Knock School District, which included the villages of Knock, Swordale and Aignish, did not fare much better with 44 servicemen killed out of 202 on active service. A horror statistic from this district records that 8 out of 9 navymen were drowned on the "Iolaire".

One remarkable hero, Leading Seaman Malcolm Macleod R.N.R. from 5 Knock, received a £50 bonus for sinking a German submarine in the Mediterranean. Sadly, Malcolm was lost in action whilst serving on SS Mereddio.

One of the most decorated servicemen from this area was Lieutenant John Munro from 27 Aignish, who was awarded the Military Cross for his "conspicuous gallantry and devotion to duty" in France. He was also awarded the prestigious Mons Star. Lieutenant Munro was also one of the most important Gaelic poets of the twentieth century. He wrote his poetry as Iain Rothach and one of his most important poems was entitled "Ar Gaisgich a Thuit 's a Bhlàr" (Our Heroes who fell in Battle). The poem speaks of death, sacrifice and foreboding but with contemplative serenity rather than anger. Lieutenant Munro was killed in action on the 16th April 1918.

The war efforts of the servicemen from this district were recorded by Donald Morrison, Headteacher of Knock Public School, but he did not specify casualties on a village basis as recorded in the other school districts.

The "Loyal Lewis" Roll of Honour includes much fascinating additional information that is not possible to include in a short article of this nature. The document can be viewed in the Stornoway Library for those wishing to undertake further research into World War 1.

Iolaire Monument, Holm

Liz Chaplin

HMY "Iolaire".
Photograph from
www.sheshader.com

THE IOLAIRE TRAGEDY - 1ST JANUARY 1919

Alasdair Macleod

The 1st of January 1919 has often been called the blackest day in the history of the island of Lewis on account of the Iolaire disaster when the Admiralty yacht the H.M. Iolaire sank at the notorious Beasts of Holm near the entrance to Stornoway harbour and 205 servicemen perished.

The ending of the war in late November 1918 brought mixed emotions from rejoicing that the struggle was over to sadness for the great loss of life in the carnage of war. As New Year approached many Hebridean servicemen made for Kyle of Lochalsh, the departure port for the Minch crossing to Lewis. However, inadequate provision had been made by the Admiralty for the numbers of returning servicemen desperate to get home for New Year. By New Year's Eve, over 500 soldiers, sailors and other military personnel were gathered on the pier but the regular mail steamer, the Sheila, was unable to take all on board. The Admiralty yacht, the ill-fated Iolaire, was called into action and set off across the Minch with an estimated 260 naval ratings and a crew of 23.

The Iolaire made it across the stormy Minch but within sight of the lights of Stornoway harbour disaster struck in the shape of the cruel outcrop of rocks known as the Beasts of Holm. When the Iolaire struck the rocks there were attempts to lower the ship's lifeboats but without success due to the ferocious state of the sea. Many of the sailors attempted to swim for the shore but the huge waves and strong undertow took their toll. Most of those who made it to safety owed their lives to the strength and bravery of John F. Macleod from Port of Ness. This stalwart seaman jumped from the boat with a heaving line and managed to reach the rocks where he then wedged himself among the boulders on the beach. The hawser which he hauled ashore was literally the lifeline along which most of the survivors managed to crawl. An estimated 205 sailors lost their lives in this horrendous tragedy and the scene of devastation round the Beasts of Holm that New Year's morning is impossible for us to imagine.

POINT COASTAL PATH

A complete circuit of The Eye Peninsula, Isle of Lewis

Tom Clark

Although the total distance of about 20 miles (33 kilometres) could feasibly be completed in two days by a fit walker, it is recommended that the walk be tackled in five easy sections, to allow time for visiting the many historic sites and other places of interest en route. The sections can be tackled in either direction, as separate walks, or in sequence, as each begins and ends at an easy access point where cars can be parked. The walk follows the shoreline (mainly clifftops) all the way, and presents no major difficulties, although there are a few scrambles (e.g. the ravines at the mouths of the Dibidale and Mill Burns in Garrabost), some areas of long heather, one or two boggy patches and one or two fences to climb over. Mainly, however, there are stiles or gates where croft or grazings boundaries obstruct the path. Some sections, such as the Aignish shoreline from the site of the old 'temple' on Chicken Head to the Braighe, and the stretch from Shulishader to Portnaguran have clearly marked footpaths with no obstructions. More information about the geographical and historical features of the Point coastline can be found in the encyclopaedic Appendix 4 of Calum Ferguson's 'Soolivan' (2004).

Please note that because much of the walk is across croft land and common grazings, dogs should not be taken.

Path towards Chicken Head   *Lewis Shand*

Sheshader Bay   *Tom Clark*

1. Sheshader - Bayble: distance 3.5 miles (6 kms), time 2hrs. 30 mins

From the Sheshader slipway, heading south, follow the left (seaward) side of the croft fences towards the first headland, Rubha na Greine or An Grianan (the green meadow). There are some fine examples of lazybeds on top of An Grianan. Follow the cliffs round to the scenic bay (Norabhaig) and cross the stile at the inner grazings fence. The path keeps close to the cliffs here, so care is necessary. Ahead is the imposing bulk of Dun Dubh (Rubha Dubh Sheshader, known locally as 'Black Sandy'), one of the highest points on the Point coastline. Cross the fence at the stile. The climb to the top is steep in places but is well worth the effort. The summit, on which can be traced the foundation of an ancient dun, or fort, affords spectacular panoramic views on a clear day of the mainland mountains, Skye, the Shiants and the north of Lewis.

On the descent of Black Sandy take care not to get too close to the sheer cliffs on the south side, then follow the cliff-tops towards the next headland, Rubha na Beiste. There is some long heather in this area which impedes rapid progress, but it is worth a short detour inland to see the dark, lonely Loch Innis. Cross the Sheshader outer boundary fence and head back to the cliffs. This section affords some amazing views of the multi-coloured contorted rock strata, mainly Lewisian gneiss, one of the oldest and hardest rocks in Europe. The walking is easier now. Continue close to the high cliff-tops past the imposing headlands of Rubha nam Bearnach (Limpets' Headland) and Rubha na Banntraich (Widow's Point), where a Bayble woman in the past is reputed to have waited for days for the return of her husband who had been drowned at sea.

Some scrambling is necessary to cross the deep cutting that marks the start of the Bayble inner grazings and crofts, but the boundary fence is well back from the edge and walking is straightforward apart from a couple of fences which go right to the cliffs.

Just before reaching the headland Rubh' a'Chaise, there is a spectacular example of a blow-hole, Toll na Roin (Seals' Hole), where the force of the sea inside a cave has blown a huge hole through to the surface inland. The resultant chasm is very deep with sheer sides, so should be approached with caution. The narrow neck of land on the seaward side can be crossed with care, but the best views of the bottom of the hole are from the far (inland) side, where the sea's intrusion can be seen far below. The big island just off the headland is known as Eilean a' Chaise (Cheese Island), but is more likely to be originally Eilean a' Chais (Sorrow Island). Just inside the bigger island is a small tidal island known as Eilean na Mairbh (Island of the Dead), where the remains of a building and some bones and pottery have been found, suggestive of possibly a monk's cell or other early Christian site. The old name for the shingle beach immediately to the north of Bayble pier was Papastaidh (Monk's Place) and the Gaelic name of Bayble itself is Pabail; both suggest early Celtic religious sites. (For further information, Google 'The Papair Project'). Follow the easy path round to Bayble pier via the new mooring basin at Papastaidh to complete this section.

Toll na Roin, Bayble   *Tom Clark*

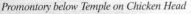

Bayble Beach   *Janet Cameron*

2. Bayble - Braighe: distance 5 miles (8 kms), time 3 hours

From Bayble pier follow the road round the south side of the beach and cross the stile at the end. Keep to the left of the double fence otherwise you will be taken in the wrong direction! Follow the cliffs round to Rubha na Strainaich which affords an unusual view of Bayble Island, looking down from above. From this point, the walk along high cliffs towards Chicken Head is magnificent, with a clearly marked sheep-path on springy spray-washed turf, and amazingly colourful and convoluted rock formations below you all the way. Also visible on this stretch are several waterfalls, sea-caves and natural arches. Shortly after passing An Chrotach (the Hunchback), a high stac favoured by sea anglers, an interesting ruin comes into

Aignish Beach   *Simon Riley*

view. Known locally as the Temple, it is reputed to be the site of one of the three earliest churches in Point, but another tradition claims it was the home of a brother and sister who were banished from the village. Again the Papair Project website provides more information. The outline of a building can be clearly seen, and there seems also to be a square perimeter wall possibly enclosing a graveyard or garden. It is a fine spot to stop for a rest, with a waterfall and a steep and slippery descent leading to a narrow ridge running out to sea, complete with sheep-path along the top. Do not be tempted to try it for yourself!

Aignish Beach   *Simon Riley*   *Foundations of old Temple on Chicken Head Tom Clark*

Shulishader Shore looking north   *Tom Clark*

From the Temple, follow the edge of the wide plateau round Chicken Head, another reputed site of an early Celtic Christian community. In fact, the name 'Chicken Head' or Aird Chirc may be an early cartographer's error for the Norse 'kirkja', a church. This headland, the most southerly in Point, affords further superb views towards the entrance to Stornoway harbour and the east coast of Lewis. Round the corner, the village of Swordale comes into view and the nature of the cliff scenery changes. The underlying gneiss gives way to much softer rock, conglomerates and boulder clay, and there is evidence of much erosion as you follow the deeply indented, precipitous coastline. Keep to the seaward side of the village grazing and croft fences and follow the coast round to Ramadal where the Knock slipway is located, then follow the EC-funded marked path round to the Braighe. This last section is longer than it looks, and you will be tired when you reach the gate at the end of this walk!

3. Braighe - Garrabost: distance 3 miles (5 kms), time 2 hrs 30 mins

At the east end of the Braighe causeway is a path to St Columba's (Ui) Church, described by local historian Colin Scott Mackenzie as 'without doubt the most significant surviving ancient building in Lewis'. Originally a cell of Catan, from the time of Columba, and later the principal church for the whole of Stornoway Parish, which included Point, the ruins have recently been restored to a safe condition and are open again to the public. Inside are the tombs of several of the early Macleod chieftains and many other prominent citizens are buried in the cemetery, although sadly some of the inscriptions are no longer legible. For further information, see the excellent 'St Columba's Ui Church' by Colin Scott Mackenzie (2012).

From the Broad Bay side of the old Ui Church, follow the clear path skirting Aignish village round the shoreline (some sections are on the village coastal road). The coastline here is subject to much more erosion than the eastern cliffs, and you are soon in the area of Garrabost clay, used to manufacture the distinctive local red bricks in the mid-19th century. The land here is much more fertile, and was made into a productive dairy farm by Lord Leverhulme, until the local crofters rebelled and took back their land during the famous Aignish Riots, commemorated by a monument adjacent to St Columba's Church. There are also some well-preserved examples of the old turf and drystone dykes, or walls, which delineate the village grazings' boundaries, and further on the old lazy-beds are distinctly laid out in long parallel ridges.

At the mouth of the Dibidale Burn, formerly used to power the Garrabost Mill, the strong-flowing stream has carved a deep ravine which requires some careful scrambling to cross. Once negotiated, continue round the cliffs with Stac Mor Garrabost to your left. Climb round the edge of the Garrabost grazings towards the twin promontories of West and East Roisnish flanking each side of a sandy bay at the foot of high cliffs. From this point on there are superbly well-preserved examples of the old lazy-bed system of cultivation, with the parallel ridges running in a herring-bone pattern right to the edge of every headland.

This stretch of coastline is very rugged, with numerous offshore rocks and tidal reefs, and

Geodha nan Eathraichean   *Tom Clark*

caves and natural arches round every corner. On one headland, An Dun Mor, there is the foundation of an ancient fort, again surrounded by lazy-beds. From here follow the coast round to the steep slipway at the end of the Manse road, the end of this section.

4. Garrabost - Portnaguran: distance 4 miles (6.5 kms), time 3hrs 30 mins

From the slipway at the end of the Manse road in Garrabost turn right, and the first challenge is to cross the deep ravine carved though the soft rock by Allt na Muilne, the Mill Burn. When the burn is full there are strategically placed stones slightly upstream to assist the crossing, then clamber up the steep northern side. The coastline here is fairly rugged, and rapid progress is impeded in places by tussocky grass, but once across the Shulishader fence the path is marked by posts with yellow stripes all the way to Portnaguran.

Once round the next headland, Gob Hunisgeir (Seabirds' Rock), there are several little bays surrounded by high cliffs including Geodh' an Uillt where the Shader Burn enters the sea, the ravine easily crossed by a sturdy bridge, and Geodha nan Eathraichean, (Boats' Gully), where the village boats were based during the fishing season. A steep stone stairway of 88 steps leads right down to the beach where the mooring places for the boats can be seen, along with two deep caves. This beautifully sheltered little anchorage is well worth a visit.

The walking from here on is pleasant and straightforward, with the low, rocky shore of Broad Bay to the left and a clearly marked path round the edge. About a mile inside the Portnaguran common grazing land, close to the shore, a scattered pile of rocks indicates the site of an ancient chambered cairn where the outlines of stone kists, or burial chambers, can be clearly seen. This site is known locally as Caisteal Mhic Creacail (Nicolson's Castle), suggesting the stones from the cairn were used at one time to build a residence for the local landowner.

Over the next rise the remains of a wrecked trawler, the Wyre Law, are prominent, high on the rocky shore. This boat, from Fleetwood, ran aground here in 1952 in a storm but all the crew were saved. The sea is gradually reclaiming what remains of the hull, and only the bow section is left intact. From here continue round the shoreline into the village of Flesherin, where a deep indentation created by Allt Chailligeadh, which drains from Loch an Duin, necessitates another scramble across. On the other side a fence must be crossed (another gate or stile needed here!) before continuing round the rocky shoreline to join the main road beside the old boathouse. From here an easy walk on the road takes you to Portnaguran pier.

5. Portnaguran - Sheshader: distance 5 miles (8 kms), time 4 hours 30 mins

This section is longer than it looks, because of the many headlands and deep indentations of the coastline, and should not be hurried in order to enjoy the many fine viewpoints and dramatic cliff scenery. From Portnaguran pier, follow the road uphill to the picnic site, then squeeze round the shoreline to the left of the fence. Beyond Geodha Sheorais another fence must be crossed (again a gate or stile would help), and then there is a pleasant, exhilarating walk round the cliffs of Cnoc Beag (Small Head) and Rubha Meadhanach (Middle Headland). From here the first views of Tiumpan Head open up, and looking south a wide panorama of the whole of the northern Eye Peninsula can be enjoyed, along with the ruined shielings of Druim Airigh an t-Siumpain in the foreground.

Camas Uinn   *Tom Clark*

Continue round the wide bay of Camas Uinn (Surf Bay), where the thundering of huge breakers on the rocky shoreline can be quite dramatic in the right conditions of wind and tide. There are quite a few caves round this bay, one known as Toll nan Ceardan, used by tinkers in olden times. Round the next small headland and the Geodha Rudha the imposing cliff face of Tiumpan Head looms ahead, and a stiff climb to the top is rewarded by another superb high viewpoint. An old wartime lookout post contains a sheltered picnic table, an ideal spot for a lunch break, overlooking the lighthouse and the whole of the North Minch. From here take the path to the northern promontory of Tiumpan Head, detached from the main headland by a narrow neck of land which involves a steep descent and a scramble to the top. This natural defensive site must surely have been the location of a dun or stronghold in the distant past.

From here carefully skirt round the sloping cliff-top to the lighthouse, then from the roadside picnic table climb the stile and head back over to the cliffs. On the northern edge of the next gully, Fidegeo, leading down to the sea, are the Lighthouse Steps, used early last century for unloading supplies. Continue round the cliff edge, round the high headlands of Goitelair and Foitelair, and then descend to the wide sweep of Portvoller Bay flanked by its southerly extremity, the headland of Rubha Deas. This semi-circular tour of the Portvoller foreshore takes nearly an hour, passing the village slipway, an impressive blow-hole, An t-Suil, fenced off just inland from the shore, and Sinigeadh (Swimming Gully).

The boundary between Portvoller and Aird grazings is marked by an old drystone wall and a fence which can be crossed by another stile. From here follow the high cliffs of Rubha Deas all the way round Aird grazing to the deep ravine, Geodha Mhor Seisiadar, at the mouth of the Dibidale Burn (another one!) which marks the Sheshader boundary. An impressive little waterfall bounces down the rocks where the burn enters the sea. Once across the fence a steep scramble down the side of the ravine, up the other side and across another fence leads to another section along high cliffs. Keep away from the edge, as there is a sheer drop below.

Once round the next headland, Rubha Quidinish, cross the grassy glen at Geodha an Rainich Mor (Great Bracken Gully) and then keep to the high ground to avoid a dangerous drop at the corner of Croft 1. Use the gate to enter the croft, then head down to the shore where a path leads round the bay to the village slipway, a pleasing picnic spot.

Bridge over Allt Mor Shader gully, Geodha nan Eathraichean from inside the cave   *Tom Clark*

Aerial view of Point looking west   *Chris Murray*

FURTHER READING

Angus, Stewart (1997) *The Outer Hebrides, The Shaping of the Islands*, The White House Press, Cambridge and Harris

Angus, Stewart (2001) *The Outer Hebrides, Moor and Machair*, The White House Press, Cambridge and Harris

Boyd, JM and Boyd, IL (1990) *The Hebrides: A Natural History*, New Naturalist Series, Collins, London

Buchanan, J (1996) *The Lewis Land Struggle*, Acair, Stornoway

Burgess, C (2008) *Ancient Lewis and Harris: Exploring the Archaeology of the Outer Hebrides*, Comhairle nan Eilean Siar, Stornoway

Cameron, AD (1986*) Go Listen to the Crofters*, Acair, Stornoway

Claypark Bricks Newsletter, 2006, Cnoc Dubh Residents' Association

Cunningham, P (1976) *A Hebridean Naturalist*, Acair, Stornoway

Cunningham, P (1990) *Birds of the Outer Hebrides*, Mercat Press, Edinburgh

Ferguson, Calum (2003) *Children of the Blackhouse*, Birlinn, Edinburgh

Ferguson, Calum (2004) *A Life of 'Soolivan'*, Birlinn, Edinburgh

Grant, JS (1998) *Discovering Lewis and Harris*, John Donald Publishers, Edinburgh

Grant, W (1920) *"Loyal Lewis" Roll of Honour*, 2nd edition, Stornoway Gazette, Isle of Lewis

Lawson, B (2011*) Lewis in History and Legend, the East Coast*, Birlinn, Edinburgh

Macdonald, D (1967) *Tales and Traditions of the Lews*, Mrs Macdonald, Stornoway

Mackenzie, Alexander (1882) *The History of the Mathesons*

Mackenzie, Colin S (2012) *St Columba's Ui Church otherwise Eaglais na h-Aoidhe: An Historical Perspective*, Urras Eaglais na H-Aoidhe, Isle of Lewis

Morrison, Donald (1895) *The Lewis Chemical Works*

Pankhurst, RJ and Mullin, JM (1991) *Flora of the Outer Hebrides*, HMSO, London

The Island of Lews, and its fishermen-crofters: In a letter to Hugh M. Matheson, Esq., the commissioner for Sir James Matheson, bart., of Lews (1878)

The Papar Project: www.paparproject.org.uk/hebrides1.html

Thompson, FG (1973) *Lewis and Harris*, David & Charles, Newton Abbot

Thompson, FG (1997) *Crofting Years*, Luath Press, Ayrshire

CONTRIBUTORS

Colin Scott Mackenzie, Stornoway

Colin is a native of Stornoway – of a local family and Seaforth Mackenzie blood – admittedly getting more diluted as the centuries pass. Sometime Procurator Fiscal in the Western Isles and latterly Sheriff in the Northern Isles. Local re-arranger of other writers' historical flowers - though he does claim some legal scholarship of his own.

Tom Clark, Sheshader

Tom, originally from the Borders and educated at Edinburgh University, has lived in Lewis since 1971, and in Sheshader since 1974. Now retired from 34 years teaching in The Nicolson Institute, he spends his time crofting, gardening, fishing and exploring the remote corners of his adopted island home. He is a member of several local bodies, including Point Community Council, Point Agricultural Society, Point Historical Society and Urras Storas an Rubha.

Alex John Murray, Upper Bayble

Alex John is a fourth generation fisherman, whose father, Murdo, was a survivor of the ill-fated Violas and whose grandfather, Alexander MacLeod, was skipper of the Muirneag. He spent 35 years at sea working with his brothers Alistair, Calum and others on their family boats: the 50' Venture SY 153, the 75' Ocean Gain SY 82 and the 100' steel trawler Ocean Venture SY 153 before becoming skipper / owner of the 64' Endeavour SY77.

Angus Macdonald, Swordale

Angus is a journalist and broadcaster and has returned to Swordale, with his wife Alison, after living in Inverness for 26 years. He is getting the croft back into working order and helping set up community development projects

Ali Whiteford, Garrabost

Ali developed an abiding interest in 19th century engineering as a result of growing up in Bristol, surrounded by the engineering wonders of Brunel - bridge, docks, railway and steam ship. Teaching chemistry at the Nicolson Institute for 30 years allowed him to indulge a love for the subject. The story of the Lewis Chemical Works pressed all the right buttons when the site was discovered in 1976. A book is in progress.

Carol Knott, Upper Bayble

Carol is a graduate of the University of Glasgow. She is a professional archaeologist who has lived in Bayble since 1988, and has worked extensively throughout the islands. She is also a polar specialist – working with international companies such as National Geographic as a lecturer, field guide, Zodiac driver and polar bear guard.

Graham Morrison, Garrabost

John Morrison, the last Garrabost Miller, died 2012, aged 96.

My father wrote this article on the Garrabost Mill and its times shortly after he and I renovated it as a hobby. For him this was a remembering of his own working days with Point people and his love for his craft. He was known as the Miller by many across the Island long after people had moved away from crofting. A man of faith, he would declare to his friends that his aim was ever to seek to show by his life and witness the love of his Saviour. Herein, many would say, he succeeded in abundance.

Maggie Smith, Achmore, Lochs

Maggie has been recording oral history for 20 years and preserves the island's heritage by creating themed publications. Maggie also presents some of our heritage in live theatre performance, community radio programmes and by collating community exhibitions and events.

Alasdair Macleod, Swordale

Alasdair has spent most of his working life on the island, including 17 years as Headteacher of Aird School. He subsequently worked for ten years at the Comhairle's headquarters in Stornoway in a variety of roles from Gaelic Development Officer to European Officer. He currently represents our area on the Council as one of the three Councillors for Sgire An Rubha.

Mark Macdonald, Garrabost

Mark has been interested in the wildlife of Point since spending school holidays at his grandparents' home in Upper Bayble. He lives locally with his young family and works for Scottish Natural Heritage.

Liz Chaplin, Garrabost

Liz, originally from Dumfries, moved to Garrabost in the late 1980s with her husband and four daughters. After almost 20 years of working locally in social work she is now closely involved with Urras Eaglais na h-Aoidhe, Point and Sandwick Development Trust and Urras Storas an Rubha.